D1446741

DATE DUE			

ENEMIES, FOREIGN

& WITHDRAWN

DOMESTIC:

A SEAL'S STORY

CARL HIGBIE

WITH BRANDON CARO

A POST HILL PRESS BOOK
ISBN (Hardcover): 978-1-61868-811-8
ISBN (eBook): 978-1-61868-810-1

ENEMIES, FOREIGN AND DOMESTIC
A SEAL's Story
© 2016 by Carl Higbie with Brandon Caro
All Rights Reserved

Cover Design by Quincy Alivio

Jacket photograph by Fredy Mfuko/Mission 101 Media

Certain names of places have been changed for the purposes of Operational Security.

Post Hill
PRESS

Post Hill Press
275 Madison Avenue, 14th Floor
New York, NY 10016
posthillpress.com

This book is dedicated to
Tyler "Mosquito" Trahan
and
Jan "Argo" Argonish

Special thanks to:
Guy Reschenthaler, Dennis Keegan,
Greg Czar, Paul Threatt,
JL Stermer, Matt Gallagher,
and Lauren Argenti

I always have and always will uphold my oath of enlistment, which does not end when you leave the service. My allegiance to country is listed in order of importance and it is our duty now and forever. This is why I wrote this book.

"I, Carl Higbie, do solemnly swear that I will support and defend the Constitution of the United States against all enemies, foreign and domestic; that I will bear true faith and allegiance to the same; and that I will obey the orders of the President of the United States and the orders of the officers appointed over me, according to regulations and the Uniform Code of Military Justice. So help me God."

Empowered by God and Country, I will not let our liberties be compromised. God bless America!

FOREWORD

One of the primary things I respect about Carl and why I was honored to write this foreword, is that he is the epitome of the SEALs' "never quit" attitude. Even though Carl experienced unfair adversity from within the ranks of his superiors, he was unwilling to compromise his name or his Code of Ethics to the brotherhood or our founding principles.

His team captured one of the baddest of the bad guys in Iraq (The Butcher of Fallujah) only to be prosecuted for supposedly mistreating the prisoner (literally allegedly bloodying his lip) while in their custody. From the first time I heard this story — well before I knew Carl personally — I was amazed that this prosecution of these Navy SEALs had ever gone to courts martial. While all the men were exonerated, there were some who were not satisfied that they had "punished" those involved sufficiently, and the subsequent destruction of all the SEALs' careers was done behind closed doors.

Keeping to his values, Carl published his first book *Battle on the Home Front: A Navy SEAL's Mission to Save the American Dream* to bring light to the travesties relating to the courts martial as well as other failures within our government, knowing full well the likely consequences. When the hammer fell, Carl was subjected to a politicized upper echelon who did everything they could to penalize him.

Carl was given the option to leave service early with an honorable discharge, and he took it. Shortly after accepting his honorable discharge, the Navy, displeased with Carl's public disclosure of his ordeal, attempted to downgrade his discharge. To this day I believe Carl was punished for telling the truth and refusing to back down to pressure from superiors.

True to his training as a SEAL, though, Carl refused to quit and allow others to destroy his reputation as a warrior and patriot of this nation. He fought back and won a unanimous decision from an Appeals hearing to restore his discharge to honorable.

Carl remains true to his devotion to this country, even in the face of unfair attacks from the politically correct within our society. Each of us can learn from his tenacity and willingness to fight—no matter the odds. I believe this is a "must read" in the history of the SEALs.

-Scott McEwen,
co-author of the #1 *New York Times* bestselling *American Sniper* and the National Bestselling *Sniper Elite* series

BAGHDAD - SUMMER 2007

We waited on the tarmac of Baghdad International Airport in groups of five to seven, bullshitting, throwing a football around, cleaning weapons, and doing last minute comms checks. The sun was falling fast in a cloudless desert sky as sand was kicked up by the afternoon winds, creating a haze which shrouded the city.

Two CH-47 Chinooks, tube-shaped troop carrier helicopters with rotor blades on either side of the fuselage, followed by two Blackhawk gunship escorts came in and landed near us. They cut their engines to save fuel for our INFIL while Stack delivered the warning order. Stack was a no-nonsense guy, a SEAL's SEAL, and when he spoke, all side bars came to an abrupt halt.

"We got some bad guys in a bad area where no one's been in a while. If anything happens out there, we're on our fucking own, nobody's coming to get us. Anybody wanna quit?"

We all laughed. This was a joke that harkened back to our days at Basic Underwater Demolition School when we were put through a grueling physical training regimen and exposed to extreme weather conditions. There were only two ways out of BUD/S: quit or conquer. Of the nearly forty or so SEALs massed up on the tarmac, nobody wanted to quit. Not then. Not now.

Stack went on to tell us that we were headed to Shirin, a small city in Southern Iraq, north of Basra, on Iran's western border, to capture a high-value target, bring him back to Baghdad and turn him over to Intel. Simple enough. Go there, get the guy, bring him back. It was possible to execute the operation without firing a single shot. I'd been on capture missions before that had gone off without a hitch.

"Anyone got anything they wanna add?"

"I just wanna say, men..." Bob, our commanding officer, interjected. "This one's for all the marbles, this is the big Kahuna, for God's sake, be careful out there!"

It was all we could do to keep from rolling our eyes and laughing out loud. Old Bob. He meant well.

This was my first deployment, and SEAL Team 10's first push back in the fight since the Operation Red Wing disaster in which eleven SEALs were killed, not to mention eight Special Forces soldiers and two Marine aviators, leaving Marcus Luttrel as the battle's lone survivor. Needless to say, there was apprehension from the leadership on down.

At almost forty, this was an unusually large number of operators for any kind of engagement, let alone a capture mission, and we chalked that up to the brass wanting to maintain control and also to get some trigger time. But the great irony was that the older SEALs—the Team 10 headquarters element that came up in the 80s and 90s during Grenada and Panama and Desert Storm—were far-removed from the operational side of things, and were more likely to be liabilities than assets on the op due to being out of the operational game for so long.

As the sun dropped out of sight, the birds commenced spinning their blades, and our large group of SEALs began boarding the two Chinooks. The Blackhawks were only there to provide escort to just beyond the Baghdad city limits, after which it would be just the two 47s heading south and slightly east. We would not rendezvous with our AC-130 gunship escort until we were a few minutes out from the insertion point. I got on the second one and settled in for the flight. The lights of Baghdad faded behind us as we moved into open desert.

It was a somber ride. No one said anything. Most of us had our headphones on blasting Metallica or Slayer. It was almost impossible to hear over the drone of the rotor blades, anyway.

Ninety minutes in and we'd arrived at the insertion point. We made a lip landing—the back of the aircraft touching down just long enough for us to disembark—while everyone stayed on a knee as the helos trailed off. We sat there for a few minutes taking in our surroundings while our point man plotted his route. Alone in the desert, contemplating the threat of gunfire or barking dogs that might give away our position; we held fast to the sand, then assembled into our respective groups and began the patrol.

There was a forward element, a rear element, two wings and a command and control element in the center, all spread out across a surface area roughly the size of a football field. I was on the left wing with ten other SEALs, give or take.

We were dropped approximately six klicks west of the target, far enough away that they wouldn't see us coming. The sand was a fine powder, like moon dust, that formed impressions of our boots as we moved silently through the desert.

We had all donned Night Optical Devices, or NODs, and the light from the city shone in the distance through our grainy lenses. It took about an hour and a half before we saw the first housing structures and the large highway that bordered Shirin to the West. We massed up on the edge of the highway, our own Rubicon. We would inevitably be spotted crossing it; the giant street lamps overhead would expose us.

We bisected the highway, bounding overwatch — one fire team at a time sprinting full tilt while the rest held defensive positions and observed for enemy activity until the initial group made its way to safety and the next team went ahead. The highway was deserted save for a lone car every one or two hundred meters, and it was less than five minutes before the whole attack force was across the highway and inside of Shirin proper.

Bob spotted a guy observing us with binoculars, but said, "Don't engage." By this time, much of the townsfolk who were comprised largely of men of military age had been made aware of our presence. We heard the occasional shouting in Arabic; the tension was extremely high.

A mixture of fear and adrenaline surged through my body. The challenge was keeping a level head, holding off on engaging the many threats that were running up and down the streets, shouting at us. We all knew that once shots were fired in earnest, all bets were off; no great battle plan survives the first shot.

The city featured a rundown urban center with dilapidated apartment buildings and streets that ran East to West, North to South, forming a grid, like a smaller Manhattan. Our target was three blocks east of the highway. We remained in our original groups and approached at a light jog, using the same bounding overwatch patrol order.

When we reached the target building, the capture team entered and my group held cordon on the southwest corner of the block. The other groups covered the remaining three street corners, and another covered the entrance to the building.

The capture team cleared the house quickly and began the initial search. A few minutes later, we heard the rip of automatic gunfire. Milky, a fellow new guy, came over the radio and said, "Hey guys, all good. Just shot some shithead in a car driving toward us, but I think you better hurry up in there, over."

Across the block we heard a few pops of an AK, so we dove behind a parked car for cover. This was the drip before the flood gates opened.

Because I was one of the assistant Joint Terminal Attack Controllers (JTAC) on the op, I was monitoring the live feed from our air assets — two fighters, a drone, and our beloved gunship — as they patrolled the airspace overhead. What I heard was alarming.

An ambush team of roughly sixty insurgents with AKs and PKM heavy machine guns were setting up on us to the North on either side of the highway. The likelihood that we could make it back to the extraction point west of the highway without engaging in a major firefight was absurdly low. If we wanted out of Shirin, we were going to have to fight our way out.

The capture team had been inside the building no longer than thirty minutes when I saw them exit through the front with the target flexicuffed and hooded. Success!

"We got him! Call it in!"

We moved with purpose through the city, block by block, until we reached the edge of the highway. Crossing over would not be as easy as it had been earlier. The first group of five thundered across as torrents of machine gun fire poured over the road, chasing them to the other side where they found cover and began returning fire. My group, the base on the east side fired as much as we could without a good view of the enemy position.

The insurgents were also east of the highway but a few blocks north. If we crossed, they would be able to fire on us directly. It was a trap, we all knew it. But there was only one way across.

I carried an MK-46, a small machine gun capable of delivering its entire 200-round drum in seconds, and when I bounded across the highway, I let them have every bit of it. Spent shells trailed me all the way to the other side.

I posted up on the corner of a small concrete structure, reloaded and continued to engage the enemy as the other Fire Teams formed a base element, making it rain shells. As the last of the guys crossed the street, Bizzle yelled for me to change positions.

"I need an automatic weapon over here!"

As I hauled ass around the corner to the new position, I tripped over a piece of rebar sticking up out of an unfinished foundation and smacked my face on the concrete, damaging my Nods and splitting my nose open.

Bizzle pulled me up and said, "You good, dude?"

"Yeah, I'm fine. Gimme a sec."

We took up positions behind a small house and continued to lay down suppressive fire against the insurgents east of the highway so the rest of the groups could bound across.

At this time, it became apparent there were more insurgents on the west side of the highway, to our north. We had taken out a lot of the shooters from the first position, but they were still firing at us. Two or three insurgents ran into a building and continued firing from inside. I hailed D-rock, the primary JTAC, who called in an airstrike that reduced the building to rubble and neutralized the threat, immediately.

With the original enemy position taken care of, I pivoted my focus to the north and began engaging the enemy there.

About twenty feet from where I stood, I saw a blast of sparks followed by a scream as Freeze fell to the ground. Bizzle ran over to see if he was okay. Freeze had brought a sniper rifle with him, which was odd, because we didn't employ him as a sniper. Lucky for him, the rifle's magazine well and his belt buckle absorbed most of the impact of the bullet. But, it still looked bad.

There was blood; it wasn't gushing, but Freeze was definitely bleeding. Doc Franky stabilized the wound with a battle dressing and made it clear we had to go, now.

Bizzle and Turtle supported Freeze from either side as we moved west into the desert. Our AC-130 gunship continued to make it rain as we hailed the helos and told them to pick us up outside the city. Once the drone of rotor blades was within earshot, our other air assets halted their campaign. The two Chinooks made full landings this time and we filed inside and were up and away in less then fifteen seconds.

I was in the bird with Freeze, who was on the verge of shock from the bullet wound, but was not in danger of losing his life. He lightened up after Doc hit him with morphine and an IV bag and we all began to laugh and talk about the op.

Bizzle chided me for falling on my ass and cracking my Nods.

"Good work, boys! No one died!"

Everyone laughed. My nose began to hurt once the waves of adrenaline wore off. When I touched it and felt how swollen it was, and how much blood had escaped, I realized it was broken. Then the pain really began to set in.

After about ten minutes everyone got quiet. Some guys closed their eyes, while others stared ahead blankly. I looked down at my legs and noticed one of my cargo pockets was torn. Stringy fibers frayed out from the seams. The pockets had been grazed by an AK or PKM round.

I pulled my pant leg up and saw tiny red scratch marks on one of my calves. They'd been caused by fragments of rounds that had burst open at my feet while I was running across the highway, firing back at the insurgent position. I ran my fingers through the torn fibers of my cargo pockets., then lightly touched my nose. It was now throbbing with intense pain, and I was reminded of a mantra I'd learned in BUD/S: "Pain is good. Pain is your friend. If you're experiencing pain, it means you're still alive."

When we landed in Baghdad there was a med team waiting for Freeze on the Tarmac and an entourage of support and intel folks awaiting our debrief, which we obliged them with once the brass had finished debating their awards.

IN THE BEGINNING

I was a tough kid to raise. I had a problem with authority. I remember getting in fist fights with classmates at school before I even learned how to read. The educators at Brunswick, the private school I attended in Greenwich, CT, weren't impressed. They tried to pacify and imbue me with a liberal-progressive philosophy, which I knew even then, was a sham. Mediocrity in all things was not only accepted, but also encouraged. When other boys teased or chided me, I was instructed by all figures of authority that I should tell the teacher. In reality, such an appeal for intervention only bolstered the resentment of my piers and gave them grounds to question my integrity. This would not do.

I learned then it was better to fight and lose than to be seen as a victim. My preferred method of conflict resolution was a two pronged approach: if insulted, I would issue a verbal warning. If the berating continued, I would strike.

My methods yielded far better results than the tell-the-teacher option. Any would-be bullies would think twice before making me the subject of their amusement, for the next week or two not because they feared reprisal from the system, but because they knew I would fight back. The administration didn't appreciate my self-reliant approach to problem solving, and I was asked to leave after I finished sixth grade. Naturally, my parents were less than thrilled and immediately turned to a reform school and medication. Who could blame them? They were surrounded by a culture that discouraged everything that I stood for and had no perspective to deal with me.

My subsequent school had me repeat the sixth grade due to poor performance in previous years. The Rectory, a reform preparatory boarding school founded along the lines of pious Protestant values, was a means of bringing me to heel. Things didn't work out that way.

At Rectory, there was an emphasis on talking about one's feelings and trying to "process" the situation when it came to conflict resolution. And there were plenty of conflicts to resolve, seeing as how many of the other kids were there for the same reasons I was. It was more of the same. I instigated my fair share of altercations against a bullying class of older boys who tested me to see how much I would put up with.

To make matters worse, my parents had sent me to a slew of mental health professionals who'd diagnosed me with everything from ADHD to Bipolar disorder and prescribed the corresponding meds.

Between the unnecessary medication, the stifling liberal-progressive dogma, and the presence of predatory older kids, it was a matter of time before things came to a head.

One time I was in wood shop just before Christmas break, and a boy two years older than me made a crack about my Hawaiian T-shirt, so I made a crack about his mom, and he didn't like that too much. He came at me swinging. I was younger and weaker and, at that point, an inexperienced fighter, so he easily got the upper hand. Desperate to get him off me, I scanned the room for a weapon. A screwdriver lay on one of the workbenches near the water fountain. I pushed the fight closer to the workbench. By now a crowd of kids had gathered and were cheering us on. Actually, they were cheering for the older kid to continue kicking my ass. I grabbed the screwdriver and plunged it into his left thigh. He cried out in horror and all the kids stopped yelling and just stood there. Needless to say, I was not asked to return after Christmas break.

My parents read me the riot act. They were good and mad, but underpinning their anger was a genuine concern about my behavior and a fear that there was something seriously wrong with me. The next evolutionary step in my treatment plan was a full-scale intensive outdoor therapeutic center in Bucksnort, Tennessee called Three Springs. The place was a cross between Outward Bound and a Maoist reeducation camp. Every night we had fire pit discussions aimed at resolving our underlying issues. The model was based on a spiritual Native American approach to healing, which was totally alien to me.

It was at my first powwow that I realized, despite my difficulties, I was in the wrong place. These other kids had serious drug problems, were clinically depressed, even suicidal. One kid had actually tried to kill both his parents. And while I recognized I had issues with authority, which made my life difficult—at times, unmanageable—I was no head case. I made up my mind then that I would do whatever was required of me and go through the motions to complete this program and matriculate to a mainstream public high school.

That Fall, I got my wish. I started my freshman year at Greenwich High School with relatively low expectations. I just wanted to be surrounded by normal kids, for once, instead of entitled douchebags or over-privileged fuck-ups who believed the world owed them something. And to my amazement, Greenwich High School turned out to be great.

I showed up for football tryouts one afternoon, weighing all of 110 pounds, soaking wet.

"You ever played before?" the coach asked me.

"No, not really."

He rolled his eyes. "Well, stand over there and watch until you figure it out."

I knew what he meant. Dejected, I walked in from the athletic field through the gymnasium where I observed the members of the wrestling team squaring off against one another.

"Am I too small?" I asked the wrestling coach, a bald man full of frenetic energy.

"Well, you look like you could fill one of our wimp weight classes, so jump on in."

I joined the others on the mat, somewhat perturbed by the coach's jab at my stature, but quickly forgot the whole thing. We did round robin takedown drills for a half hour, then the coach blew the whistle.

"Hey man, we're gonna hit the weight room. You wanna come?" a pimple-faced skater with thick glasses named Danny asked me.

"Yeah!"

We lifted weights for a couple of hours that afternoon and I got to know some of the other wrestlers. They were all just regular dudes who went to school, did their homework (mostly) and wrestled. It was a welcomed change from the basket cases and prima donnas I'd encountered at my previous schools.

Wrestling became my thing, and I was good at it. I won counties twice, states once, and was top five in New England and one of only a handful of wrestlers from GHS to ever compete at nationals.

When it came to academics, I was a mediocre student. But unlike so many from my generation, I had no delusions of grandeur about what I was capable of. I wanted to be a SEAL, and I knew, even then, that that was something I could and would achieve. And Naval Special Warfare didn't require a 4.0 grade point average.

The second or third week of my senior year, I was in gym class on the treadmill when I saw on one of the mounted TVs in the weight room the image of a plane careening into the World Trade Center, the words "Terrorist Attack" emblazoned at the bottom of the screen.

I wanted to be part of the strike force that would respond to this attack, but I still had a year of high school left. And people who are from where I'm from are expected to go to college after high school, so that's what I did, even though it's not what I wanted for myself.

The following year I attended Sacred Heart University in Fairfield, CT on a wrestling scholarship. I was invested in wrestling, at least initially, and less enthused with academic pursuit and I felt like I was wasting valuable time that could be spent in the service of my country. I commuted from my parents' house the first semester of my freshman year, but moved into campus housing the following semester.

The guys I lived with were slightly older versions of the lazy, over-privileged, undisciplined douchebags I'd known my whole life. I did not want to be like them.

My interest in wrestling began to wane and my grades started slipping after the first semester. The school thing was not for me, at least not at that point. The breaking point came when I received an F on a critical response paper I'd written for my English class. I went to speak to the professor about my grade, but he brushed me off.

"Maybe college isn't for you, Carl."

Maybe you're right, dickhead.

I drove directly to the Navy recruiter's office in nearby Bridgeport, sat down across from him and said, "I'm gonna be a SEAL, I need you to do all the paperwork."

"Well, let's get started then," he said after a second, once he realized I wasn't joking.

We spent a couple of hours dotting the i's and crossing the t's and at the end I said, "Okay, I'm ready to go now, I'll just have to run home and grab a few things."

"Hahahaha, no Carl. You won't ship out till April. But we can go to MEPS in Springfield tonight and you can sign your contract tomorrow."

"April? What the fuck? I'm ready to go now!"

"I know you are, but the Navy won't be ready for you till April."

"I don't understand, the US just declared a War on Terror and I have to wait till fucking April to ship? That seems kind of inefficient."

He looked at me sheepishly and said, "Yep."

Flanders was his name. Fire Controlman First Class Flanders. He was definitely not a SEAL.

About an hour later, after we'd finished up the requisite paperwork, we drove back to my house to grab a few things for the overnight stay at MEPS and break the news to my parents.

When we got there, only my mom and two younger sisters were home.

"Buddy, what is going on?" my mom inquired, puzzled at the presence of a man in naval uniform in her house.

"Done with school, going to be a SEAL now," I said, rushing to get my things together.

"We'll talk about this later, Bud," she said in a concerned tone.

"Nothing to talk about, Mom. I've made my decision."

Tears welled up in her eyes and she left the room abruptly. Flanders just stood there awkwardly. He told me later he'd seen this scenario played out a hundred times before.

★

Flanders dropped me off at the MEPS station in Springfield, MA where I stayed the night in a military hotel. The following morning I was put through a battery of aptitude and vocational tests and medical screenings to make sure I was fit for full duty. In the afternoon I met with a detailer, the person responsible for assigning orders, and signed over six years of my life to Naval Special Warfare. If, for some reason, I were unable to complete any part of SEAL training, I would be relegated to the Fleet, henceforth to be known as a "wash-out," and made to swab the deck and scrub the toilets. I shuddered at the thought.

Flanders picked me up and drove me back home where he explained to both my parents what a brave young man I was and how proud they should be and how most of the kids from my generation were dirtbags, but not me! There was tension at the dinner table after he left.

"I really wish you would just finish out the year at school," my dad said imploringly.

"Dad, I didn't even want to go to college in the first place, but I did it because I thought it was what you wanted. It's just not for me, and I feel I have a lot more to offer as a SEAL than as a college student." After some more bickering, I put my fork down, said good night, and went to my room. No one bothered me the rest of the evening.

A few days later, out of anger, I was speeding on wet roads and totaled my parents' '99 Ford Explorer by driving it into a tree. I was so pissed at myself, and all I could think was, *Holy shit. If my parents didn't hate me before, then they are definitely going to hate me now.*

Being out of school and having no job and nothing really planned for the next seven months left me feeling pretty worthless. Thankfully I had a close friend who hooked me up with a sweet '89 VW station wagon.

From his house, I went to see another friend of mine named Rick, who owned a boatyard down the street, and I asked for a job until I shipped off to the Navy. Rick introduced me to another guy named Jan Hansen, who at the time was renting a corner of the boatyard. Though Jan was about twenty years older than me, we hit it off pretty well. Jan is one of the most honest, hardworking, and genuine people I have ever met. He owned a small marine construction company that did dock-building, renovation, and salvage work in the area. The work was great. It paid well and I could work outside. It was the perfect job until I shipped out to boot camp. Also, hearing that I was home, my high school wrestling coach and longtime role model, Brad Wallace, asked me if I wanted to be the assistant coach in the evenings. Of course as a former LL (the largest high school division) state and two-time county champ, I was more than happy to accept.

For the next six months, I worked hard from 5:00 AM to 2:00 PM on the barge with "Jan Han" as I called him. Then I spent 2:30 to 6:00 PM with Brad at wrestling practice, Monday through Friday. Usually Jan and I would work weekends, too, for a few hours, just to stay caught up with the endless work load.

I had also been introduced to a local SEAL reservist. He ran a program that helped get recruits ready for the initial screening test prior to the kick in the nuts we were volunteering for called BUD/S (Basic Underwater Demolition school), the preliminary seven-month screening to becoming a SEAL. Soon after showing up at the first training session of his prep course, I was told that I would not make it through the training and would not receive his recommendation at BUD/S. *Whatever*, I thought.

As the end of March came around, I started making the preparations for my departure. I told Jan that I was done, said my good-byes, and tied up any loose ends before officially entering the Navy. Of course, I would never have left without a massive going-away party. With the help of my good friend Joe, I organized a gathering of friends and friends of friends, and whoever else, and got ahold of six kegs. The guy whose house it was, an older guy named Box, (not sure if that was his real name or not) immediately regretted his decision to let me host the party at his house when he saw us bringing in the kegs. But I paid him $500, plus the cost of a cleaning service, so all was well in the end.

It was April 4, 2004, and while waiting in my parents' kitchen for the recruiter to arrive and take me away, my mother asked me, "Bud, are there any more guns, knives, explosives, or any other potential contraband in the house?"

I ran upstairs to rifle through my secret caches and found one more two-pound Pyrodex and ammonium nitrate pipe bomb with a thirty-second fuse on it. I came trotting down the stairs with it in my hand, intending to detonate it in the back yard before I left. By this time, the recruiter had arrived and was explaining to my parents how I was making an honorable decision and blah, blah, blah, the usual bullshit they say to help themselves sleep at night after dishing out all the lies they tell you to get you to join.

My entrance into the room with the equivalent of a little over a pound of TNT was a little shocking to the recruiter but was business as usual to my parents. My mom proceeded to tell me that we should give it to the police and they would take care of it. I laughed, as I knew I had them in a leveraged position, and said, "Mom, right now the best thing for all of us is for me to set it off and pretend it never happened — what do ya say?"

"Okay, but I hope it's not too loud," said my dad reluctantly. I grabbed a lighter and walked outside, instructing everyone to stay indoors. I lit it and threw it over the stone wall about forty yards from the back of the house. This was not my first rodeo, so I ran inside pretty quickly.

Thirty seconds or so of silence went by, which was broken by an earth shattering BANG that shook the pictures on the wall and launched nearly a cubic yard of dirt over two hundred feet in the air. Going forward, my life would be replete with similar explosions, both in training and in combat.

I bid my farewells to my family and departed. As we drove down the driveway, I shed a tear. Not really sure what I was upset about, I turned around and looked at the recruiter whose white-knuckled fists were wrapped around the steering wheel just in time for him to tell me, "I think you'll fit in just fine at BUD/S."

Boot camp was a miserable experience that taught me nothing useful except the ranking system and how to fold clothes the Navy way. Immediately after graduation, I was off to "A" school. Everyone in the Navy prior to going to BUD/S had to pick a job, because of the high attrition rate. This way, if a SEAL candidate quit or failed, the Navy could put them right to work in the fleet. I picked SK (Store Keeper) for a rate or job title, because it had the shortest school term and got me to BUD/S the fastest. This was another month of my life I will never get back. It was truly amazing that these fat slobs at the schoolhouse who sat behind desks and ordered whatever needed to be ordered held themselves in such high esteem. It occurred to me that this particular schoolhouse sought out the worst of the fleet, removed them from operational jobs and put them here where they could do the least amount of damage.

For example, every morning we had group workouts prior to classes, which usually consisted of a total of five or ten sets of ten pushups mixed in with an equal number of sit-ups and jumping jacks, followed by no more than a two-mile run at just over a walking pace. The same instructor always led the Physical Training (PT) while the other instructors walked around hassling the class because they were too fat or out of shape to keep up.

One day on one of these "runs," I spoke up and asked if I could do PT on my own because I was in training for BUD/S and this program was hurting my training. This was met with serious criticism. One of the instructors said, "If you think you can do a better job, why don't you lead PT tomorrow morning?" Confused as to whether this was meant to be a punishment or not, I accepted. The next morning, I was amped and ready for a good workout. I kicked off the set with a quick warm-up, followed by ten sets of progressively more intense sprints. We then broke the one-hundred-person group into five stations of pushups, sit-ups, lunges, pull-ups, and fireman carry squats. Even before the first rotation was complete, the same instructors who asked me to lead PT stepped in and shut it down. Apparently this twenty-five-minute workout was too intense for a bunch of "soldiers." I was instructed to skip over to the run, which I extended to three miles at a reasonable eight-minute pace. Wrong again. Less than half a mile into the run, I was reprimanded by the panting instructor who had been struggling to keep up and moved to the back of the pack so the regular instructor could take over. "A" school was a joke, I couldn't wait to get out of there. I took a short leave and went home to visit with friends and family before reporting for duty at BUD/S.

It was now August, and I had just landed in San Diego, California. I waited on the curb in my dress whites for the duty driver to pick me up and take me to the compound where I would live for the next seven months. Some guy who had washed out showed up and told me to get in. The drive over was short, but I was all too ready to begin my real journey. He walked me across the grinder (a square, paved area surrounded by pull-up bars and BUD/S related offices) where a number of helmets lay on the ground. The helmets belonged to men who had tried and failed to make it through BUD/S. One of them had previously belonged to the driver.

He said, "Don't be one of those guys." I didn't say anything, but kept walking to the quarterdeck. No sooner had I walked through the door than a BUD/S instructor started yelling at me, insisting that I go get wet and sandy. I smiled and hauled ass to the ocean, over the fifteen-foot sand berm and into the fifty-five-degree water. On the way back, I dove into the sand and rolled till I was covered head to toe. The tiny grains dug into my skin, which caused the sensation of chafing. It is a sensation that will be with me for all time.

I made it back to the same instructor as fast as I could and stood at attention. I had never been so proud. Here I was, about to start the most elite military training in the world; nothing could bring me down.

What can be said of BUD/S that hasn't already been expressed or portrayed in the myriad TV shows and Hollywood movies about our community? It was cold, it was wet, it was sandy. We chafed. The next seven months were about as challenging as could be. And whenever I thought it couldn't get any harder, it did, over and over again. Everyone who was there for the right reasons all had the same mentality. We were there because we wanted to be top-level operators, not because we had something to prove to ourselves or to see if we had it in us. We knew we had it in us; there was never a question.

Graduation from BUD/S came, that same reserve captain who said I wouldn't make it showed up and was quick to declare, "I always knew you'd get through." The next day everyone shipped off to Army jump school at Fort Benning, the next phase in the pipeline. Jump school was three weeks that could have been made into three days; leave it to the military to drag things out. It has since been truncated to a weeklong course for SEALs. After graduation, we started SQT (SEAL qualification training), the final step to becoming a Navy SEAL.

TEAM 10

June 29, 2005. Just another day at SQT, the training period directly following BUD/S. We were in the classroom dicking around, bullshitting, awaiting education via PowerPoint. An instructor entered the room and dropped it on us; no one saw it coming.

"Everybody shut the fuck up." The room went quiet. "Echo Platoon just lost a bunch of SEALs in Afghanistan," he continued. "Another four are missing in action. We need volunteers to go on stand-by."

As though by muscle memory, and before I could even wrap my head around what the instructor had just said, my hand shot into the air and held there. A few others raised their hands as well, about half the class.

"Good." The instructor took our names down in a mini notepad. "Training's cancelled today."

"What the fuck happened?" Lenny blurted out.

"I don't have all the particulars, but apparently a four man recon team got into a fire fight in the mountains out there, and reached out for help. A 47 with eight SEALS and eight Special Forces guys on board got shot down by an RPG or something. The details are a little fuzzy. All you need to know is that we need bodies."

He made eye contact with all the volunteers, nodded his head and stepped out of the room. We young SEAL pups were left to chew the fat. The room was silent at first. We knew that SEALs can be killed; that's an unfortunate feature of our job. And yet, up to that point, we didn't truly believe it. We understood it in the abstract the way most people do. But this was different. This was real.

"Eight fucking SEALs! Jesus Christ!" Beads gasped finally.

"And another four MIA, plus the eight other guys!" I responded. "That's gotta be one of the worst days in SEAL history."

We didn't know it then, but the mission the instructor had alluded to was Operation Red Wing, and of the four SEALs missing in action at the time of our briefing, only one, Marcus Luttrell, would live to tell the tale. His memoir,

Lone Survivor, was published in 2007, and later adapted into a feature film.

We were busy with advanced dive training at the time this all went down. Ordinarily, we would have received the lesson of the day that morning, broken for lunch, then spent the remaining four to six hours underwater completing various tasks, navigating, and building and taking apart mock charges.

With training cancelled, I made straight for the barracks to pack a go-bag. A flurry of excitement and anxiety washed over me. This was it, my number had been called. The next three days as we volunteers awaited further orders, we took to training once more, though it was nearly impossible during this time to stay focused and present. My thoughts wandered inexorably to the Afghan countryside. I wondered what it must feel like to be torn apart by bullets or blown to bits by mortar rounds. I thought about the men who'd died fighting; how brave they were. I wondered how many Taliban fighters they'd taken down with them. I wondered, too, how many I might have been able to take down had I been in the fight.

On the third day we received word that Echo Platoon, having sustained a significant reduction in the number of experienced operators within its ranks, was being swapped out with Foxtrot Platoon, effectively nullifying our volunteer assignment orders.

Frustrated yet somewhat relieved, I threw myself into training with a renewed vigor and strengthened resolve, that, should I ever find myself downrange, surrounded, out gunned or out flanked, I would and will fight to the last breath.

After SQT we received our tridents; the unmistakable gold rendered eagle clutching a pistol by the barrel with one talon, and Poseidon's scepter with the other that crosses over an anchor. These warfare devices are worn above the left breast pocket of all working and dress uniforms. With utility and camouflage uniforms a patch in the SEAL trident design is stitched into the fabric for more practical application.

Receiving my trident, or bird, as we called them, was one of the proudest moments of my entire life. Enshrined in this talisman was the warrior spirit of the fighting Frogmen who have gone before me, the recognition of my peers that I have survived and mastered this gauntlet of initiation and now stand among them; a testament to my total and absolute commitment to the defense against all enemies, foreign and domestic, of the United States of America.

Upon graduation, our official orders were disseminated. We cued up outside the personnel office, each man eager and rambunctious to receive his first assignment as a SEAL.

"Higbie! Get in here!"

"Moving, Masterchief!"

I entered the Masterchief's office per his request. It was a simple room, a few books on shelves, photos on the wall of what I imagined was Bosnia or Kosovo in the mid-1990s. In each of them a wiry Masterchief (who was clearly not a Masterchief at the time the pictures were taken) stood beside fellow SEALs grinning ear to ear, a loaded M16 supported at the grip by his right hand. In some of them, giving a thumbs up with his left.

"You're going to Team 10, Carl."

"Echo Platoon?"

"They'll assign you a platoon once you check in, but if I was a bettin' man, I'd say Echo is where you'll end up. You taking any leave days?"

"Just a few. I'm going to head home to Connecticut to pick up my car, maybe stop at Penn State to see my sister, then head down to Little Creek."

I caught Beads's eye as I exited the room. He'd been just behind me in the cue. I mouthed the words "Team 10" and smiled.

"Beads!" The Masterchief shouted. "Get in here."

"Moving, Masterchief!"

We left Coronado for Alaska to complete cold weather training: land navigation and marine training in sub-zero temperatures, oftentimes with low visibility on account of heavy rain or snow fall. Challenging and exciting as it was, a comparatively small number of SEALs ever actually conduct missions in conditions such as these (where there is a maritime element), leaving many to wonder if the training is indeed necessary for all SEALs to undertake. This thought often occurred to me when I was soaking wet and freezing my ass off.

To my great satisfaction, Beads was also assigned to SEAL Team 10, so we decided to trek across the country in his Jeep Wrangler. The vehicle's canvas top flapped mercilessly as we tore through the country accompanied by another SEAL who was towing the trailer we had rented with all of our stuff in it.

Chris Barton, the other guy from our class, followed along in his lifted Chevy S-10 with the trailer as far as Memphis, at which point he broke off to spend some time with his wife and kid. However, Beads and I, the young bachelors that we were, made a beeline for Penn State to party with my sister and to release whatever pent up tension we'd managed to accumulate throughout our time at Coronado and in Alaska.

The kids at Penn State didn't know what to make of us. They came at us with this bizarre mixture of gratitude and pity that we should take up the duty of fighting for our country, a country at war on two fronts. For them, there was little distinction between the actual military, and the amalgamated source of war movie vernacular and nomenclature from which they drew freely in their attempts to communicate with us.

They would say things like, "Did you see any action?" or "What's the body count like in Iraq?" Beads and I would make eye contact and burst out laughing. Or sometimes we would even play along, entertaining their uninformed notions of enemy contact and the like. At the time, we were not, ourselves, combat veterans, and knew nothing of combat other than the fact that it was a senseless thing to talk about until or unless you'd experienced it first hand, and even then, words were limited in their ability to express its nature.

But all in all, we had a great time at Penn State. They enjoyed our company, and we theirs. They were and are our countrymen, and per our oath, we are sworn to defend them. Their safety and their way of life is what we fight for. They're not supposed to know what we go through.

After our pit stop at Penn State, we arrived at my hometown of Greenwich, CT. Beads was blown away at the degree of wealth on casual display, the towering homes and groomed estates, the sheer number of Mercedes, BMWs and Porches parked along Greenwich Avenue, the East Coast equivalent of Rodeo drive.

My family loved him, they could see he was a good guy and that we were friends. But I'd be lying if I said he wasn't taken aback somewhat by his surroundings.

"Dude, you grew up *here*?" Beads asked almost in disbelief.

"Yeah," I responded, mindful of the implications.

I'm not ashamed of being born into a well-heeled family, predisposed to opportunities that are elusive to most. And I don't perceive those who are less fortunate to be low-class or untouchable. I believe that a man is what he works at, what he fights for. And I have wanted to be a Navy SEAL from the time I was old enough to play with Super-Soakers.

"Man, why would you leave this place to join the Navy?" he asked me, puzzled.

"I didn't leave to join the Navy, I left to be to a SEAL."

And with that, he understood perfectly, and we never talked about where or how I grew up again.

The few nights we spent in Greenwich were also a blast. I caught up with friends I hadn't seen since I'd left for bootcamp a year and a half earlier. We congregated at the old haunt, Davey Byrne's, in neighboring Port Chester, NY, and partied like we were still in high school.

But my friends noticed a change in me. They could tell I was more serious, more grown up possibly. And while we never spoke openly about it, I observed that they were worried they might never see me again. They'd heard about

Operation Red Wing in Afghanistan; about Markus Luttrel. And at the time, November 2005, there were soldiers and marines getting killed in Iraq left and right. SEALs too.

After a few days in Greenwich, we hit the road. It was a straight shot down I-95, then I-64 onto Little Creek, VA, headquarters of SEAL Team 10. We arrived around 3 PM, having gotten an early start that morning, and made for the quarter deck in our dress blues, as was protocol for checking into a new command. As soon as we crossed the threshold, the Petty Officer of the Watch shouted, "Cyclops!"

"What?" I said. Beads and I turned to one another, confused.

"Cyclops, you fucking retards!" he shouted. "Pick up your dicks and follow me!"

He sprinted out of the building and across the street to the bay all the while pointing toward the water and screaming, "Cyclops! Cyclops!"

Beads and I followed directly and when we reached the edge of the bay, the Petty Officer of the Watch screamed, "Well?"

Still quite unsure of what was going on, Beads and I once more locked eyes. This sent the chief overboard.

"Get in the fucking water, assholes! Go! Go! Go!"

Of course! I thought. *Cyclops means jump in the frozen bay in November in our dress blues! That makes perfect sense!*

Beads and I ran down and got ourselves soaking wet and shuffled back to the chief, who was now sporting a shit-eating grin.

"Welcome to varsity."

Directly following our baptism, we returned to the quarter deck and were led eventually to a room where six other sopping wet SEALs were sitting down, filling out paperwork and shivering mildly.

"Cyclops?" Beads inquired.

"Fucking cyclops," Lenny answered.

He'd been with us at BUD/S and SQT and in Alaska as well. In fact, almost everyone in the room were guys we'd known from training at one point or another.

After a short time in the room, a Chief came in (not the Petty Officer of the Watch) and hollered to us, "Higbie, Lenny. Come with me."

We followed him out of the room into a hallway that opened up to a wide landing of sorts. On the far wall of the landing there was an enormous mural of some faces that I had come to recognize.

"You know who they are, don't you?" asked the Chief.

"Yes, Chief," I answered.

"I do, Chief," Lenny replied.

"You aren't replacing these men, because they're *irreplacable*! You understand."

"Hooyah, Chief!" Lenny and I replied in unison.

"You've got some very big goddamned shoes to fill." He looked up in the direction of the mural depicting the men who'd been killed on Operation Red Wing. "I want you to take a good look at these guys; and whenever you're getting your ass beat in PT, whenever you're dog tired from being underwater all fucking day, whenever you're out in the fight and you're scared shitless, I want you to think about these guys and what they gave. Can you do that?"

"Hooyah, Chief!"

"Good." He smiled. "Welcome to 10."

ECHO PLATOON

When we checked in, sometime in November '05, most of Team 10 was returning from deployment to Afghanistan and guys were taking post-deployment leave to see their families and decompress. And they had a lot to decompress from; Echo Platoon alone had suffered the largest loss of SEAL life in a single day since Vietnam.

With everyone coming back home then going out on leave, the command was in flux. Headquarters was a ghost town. Lenny and I and a few other check-ins mustered every morning at 0630 on the quarterdeck because we hadn't yet been assigned to a platoon.

Some dickhead called CJ, who'd been with the Teams for five platoons, would call role, then send us all to the water

O-course. "O" was for obstacle and there was no shortage of them on this gauntlet.

The water O-course was a series of physical challenges suspended over an Olympic-size pool, 164 feet long, 82 feet wide. The path of the course ran across the pool lengthwise and reversed directions twice, creating a giant S-shape.

The sequence was as follows: starting from a three meter dive platform, Tarzan swing on a thin rope then let go in the middle of the trajectory, fly about five feet from the let-go point and grab hold of a cargo net. Climb twenty-five feet up to the top of the net, transfer to a horizontally hung rope and upside down, shimmy across fifteen feet, drop twenty-five feet into the pool, swim ten feet to the next obstacle.

Climb twenty-five feet up a thick rope; at the top of the rope is a series of suspended rings. Traverse fifteen feet across, ring from ring—jungle gym style—drop down twenty-five feet to the water, swim ten feet to the next obstacle.

Climb an orange rope ladder twenty-five feet up to the top, traverse hand-over-hand across two consecutive horizontally hung ropes that are fifteen feet in length, each. Drop down twenty-five feet, swim ten feet to the next obstacle. Change directions.

Climb twenty-five feet up a caving ladder, walk twenty-five feet across a pair of vertically parallel thin ropes, drop down twenty-five feet into the water, swim ten feet to the next obstacle.

Climb twenty-five feet up a thin rappelling rope, more jungle gym rings, then thick ropes with knots at the bottom, thirty feet across. This is a rest point (although CJ would scream at us if we stopped even for a minute). Drop down twenty-five feet to the water, swim ten feet to the next obstacle.

Climb twenty-five feet up a thick rope, go hand-over-hand across two fifteen-foot consecutive horizontally hung ropes, drop down twenty-five feet to the water, swim twenty feet to the next obstacle. Change directions.

Climb twenty-five feet up a thick rope, traverse hand-over-hand twenty feet across a steel rafter, drop down twenty-five feet to the water, swim ten feet to the next obstacle.

Climb twenty-five feet up a thick rope with knots in it, tight rope walk twenty feet across a beam, do ten front grip pull-ups, drop down twenty-five feet to the water, swim ten feet to the next obstacle.

Climb twenty-five feet up a thin rappel rope. With two pieces of PVC pipe, shimmy across a pair of horizontally parallel ropes that are slack in the middle, do ten pull-ups on the steel rafter, then do a muscle-up onto the rafter and sit. That is the last obstacle.

We were required to at least attempt this several times each morning.

If you fall during an obstacle, you have to start over from the beginning. Roughly ten percent of SEALs can complete the whole thing. My gymnastics background gave me an edge, and I was able to complete the whole course on most of my attempts. But that thing kicked my ass every time.

In a break room at headquarters where we stashed our gear in the mornings because we hadn't yet been given lockers, we loitered, shooting the shit. In the military, even in the Teams, there's a lot of downtime. The Navy is like the DMV, but with nuclear submarines. Hurry up and wait, we'd say. The day inevitably arrived that we were farmed out to the platoons.

Chief Alanzo came in and gave the assignments.

"Hizenboch, Jeffreys—Alpha. Truesdale, Jefferson—Bravo. Flannigan, Rialto—Delta. Lenny, Higbie, Gonzales, Burns, G-unit—Echo."

It made sense that Echo Platoon would get the lion's share of new operators; they needed bodies to fill in for the guys who didn't come home after Operation Red Wing.

We shuffled out of the break room and beat it upstairs to Task Unit 3 which housed the administrative offices and a common briefing room for Echo and Foxtrot platoons. (Each SEAL Team has three task units which, unto themselves, have two platoons. Task Unit 1 is Alpha/Bravo, 2 is Charlie/Delta.)

As we entered Echo platoon's office, I noticed immediately that we were being sized up by some of the veteran SEALs. We were Fucking New Guys, or FNGs, so we had yet to cut our teeth.

Of the new check-ins, at twenty-two, I was the youngest. But some of these guys that had been with the Team for two plus years were even younger than I was. Not only that, but they were significantly smaller than us as well. There was tension right from the get-go. The SEAL community isn't kindergarten, and I was willing to accept a level of hazing before I'd demonstrated my value to the platoon. But some of these smaller, younger guys were put off by us joining their platoon, and weren't shy about showing it. New guys vs. old guys became a thing.

"Oh, look at these motherfuckers!"

One in particular, a small-framed, 165-pound, cocky twenty-two-year-old from Miami that we called Rico (Suave), took it upon himself to let us know we would have to earn our keep if we wanted a place in *his* platoon.

He had no real authority, and we knew it. But he had a hard time with us from the day we were assigned to Echo. One-upmanship was his thing.

I'd later learn that Rico was one of those guys who became a SEAL for the absolute worst reason: to say he was a SEAL. Most others like him wash out by Hell Week, but some make it through. Hubris and vanity, not courage and commitment were his core values. He exemplified the type of SEAL I did *not* want to be.

A guy in his late twenties poked his head in the room and said, "Hey, I'm B-rad, your new LT. Go ahead, get settled in. Don't let any of these clowns give you too much shit."

The TEAMs have a different way of doing things from the rest of the military. We have long hair, we call our officers by their first names. We're on our own program. But we get it done, so the relaxed military standards are tolerated for the most part.

"Hey Deuce," B-rad continued. "Take these guys down to the Kill House and get 'em sorted out."

"Roger that."

Deuce was a two-platooner, meaning he'd deployed twice already with the platoon. That's why we called him Deuce. A six to eight month deployment every eighteen months is the norm. And Deuce had two under his belt. He was a salty dog.

Me, Lenny and Burns (named for a stunning likeness to the Simpsons character) were the only new guys present that day. Everyone else was at least a one-platooner.

On the way to the Kill House we stopped at the armory and drew M4s with Blue Barrels and simulation rounds; gun powder propelled paint pellets that hurt like hell.

The house was a large complex of many rooms. Each room had a door. The subject of the day's training was room clearing.

"Listen up!" Deuce hollered. "These aren't real rounds, but treat 'em as real. If you shoot me, I will fuck you up!"

"Hooyah!"

"Don't fucking 'hooyah' me, we're not in BUD/S anymore, dip shits!"

All I could think about was how much of a dick this guy was. *Is he going to act like this the rest of the cycle?* I thought.

We started with four-man stacks just outside the door. When the order was given, the first man kicked in the door, and the others moved quickly into the room and out of direct line with the doorway of death as they call it.

Each man swept his assigned corner and called out "clear." Once the whole room was cleared, we'd breach the next door. Tango targets, or enemies, would be interspersed with friendlies or hostages. If we shot a friendly, Deuce warned us, we would get fucked up.

"Do it again!" I heard a voice from above shout.

It was B-rad in the rafters with Krom, packing his perpetual dip, spitting on us if we moved too slowly or screwed up. Krom was our Leading Petty Officer (LPO). He defined professionalism. With over five platoons under his belt dating back to Kosovo, he was a beacon of knowledge.

I was fortunate enough that he took a liking to me early on, which, in the short term, caused a lot of pain, but in retrospect, probably saved my life more than once.

After a while, we got the hang of things. We could clear the whole house in under ninety seconds. This was my first day with Echo Platoon; nothing like the training pipeline. We had learned the fundamentals—weapons and tactics, fire and movement—but everything at SQT was done at a controlled pace, so that we could develop technique and build skill.

At the Kill House, it was all about speed. Speed and precision. Operational tempo. I was hooked.

We spent about four or five hours at the house. It's easy to lose track of time during training. After we secured for the day I headed back to the place I was staying—the house of a friend who I'd met at SQT. He was finishing up in Coronado, but told me I could crash there until I found a place. The Teams are pretty tight. We're there for each other.

After a few weeks, the rest of Team 10 returned from leave and the platoons were back to full strength. Echo, having lost so many men and so much talent and experience, was in a rebuilding phase. It wasn't long before we were getting started with the work-up for our subsequent deployment. We weren't sure where we'd be headed, exactly. Usually, half the team deploys to Europe or Africa to train with allied countries, while the rest goes to Iraq or Afghanistan. All we knew is that we had some serious training ahead of us. The following March we got going.

Medical

Each SEAL platoon is staffed with one to two corpsmen. A corpsman is what we call a medic in the Navy. Because our mission demands that we operate in hostile areas, possibly for long periods of time, each SEAL must be trained to the level of a basic corpsman, and each SEAL corpsman must be trained to the level of a trauma nurse.

For our first block of pre-deployment training, we went out in the woods locally, not far from Little Creek, and simulated combat casualty scenarios in which we rendered aid to wounded SEALs. The wounds, obviously, were artificial. However, the procedures we went over were the real deal.

For example, Lenny and Burns would be laid out on the ground, and I would have to low crawl to them and evaluate their injuries. If Lenny had a hemorrhage from a lower extremity (the most common cause of preventable death on the battlefield) I would tie a tourniquet around the leg, four inches above the wound, then apply a pressure dressing to the wound itself and secure it with an ace wrap. When the dressing was set, I would loosen the tourniquet, but leave it on, in case I had to retighten it in the event that the bleeding started up again.

If Burns had a sucking chest wound caused by a bullet to the torso, I would look, listen and feel for the rise and fall of his chest. If I determined that he suffered a tension pneumothorax with collapsed lung (the second most common cause of preventable death on the battlefield) I would cut open his blouse with trauma shears, apply an occlusive dressing to the wound, locate the exit wound and apply a second occlusive dressing. When he was all patched up, I would use a 14-gauge IV catheter and poke a hole in the second intercostal space — between the second and third ribs — mid-clavicle on the injured side of the chest. Once the needle punched through the chest wall, all the air trapped in the thoracic cavity would escape and the collapsed lung would be restored. We practiced this routine on trauma dummies.

After they were stabilized I would insert IVs into their veins and push fluids. Then I would simulate calling in a MEDEVAC, and while we waited, I'd reassess the treatments I'd implemented. Then we would switch and I would be the patient.

There was a feeling of disinterest that spread through the platoon because, at the end of the day, all we were doing was playing doctor. We weren't treating real life injuries;

we were acting. But what were we supposed to do, shoot a bunch of goats, patch them up and stick them with IVs?

Land Warfare

Our second pre-deployment training block took place somewhere in Arkansas. It went about five weeks. The terrain was slightly less hilly than Appalachia, but still had contour. The massive military base on which we trained was heavily wooded with brooks and streams dividing the land.

We practiced Immediate Action Drills, or IADs—small unit patrol tactics allowing for all manner of contingencies. We would patrol silently down a trail, simulate taking contact from the left, return fire, establish a defensive perimeter, and make a tactical retreat or assault. Then we would do the same thing on the right side. Then, we would add a casualty scenario, wherein one of our guys would be hit and have to be MEDEVACed out, all while under fire. And these were live fire drills; no sim rounds. Shooting and moving over vast terrain made for an interesting dynamic, one which I had, heretofore, not experienced. The complexities of calls to cover and move had to be executed at a level of perfection in order to avoid shooting another teammate.

"I'm up, they see me, I'm down" was the mantra. The exhausting series of twenty to thirty iterations of fifty-meter sprints each time we made "contact" instilled in me the confidence and competency that kept me alive on multiple deployments.

We did land navigation drills — orienteering with actual compasses — to make sure we each had a good general sense of direction. We did marksmanship training with M4 rifles and Sig pistols. We each fired various sniper rifles extensively, and did explosives training as well; mostly C4 and claymore mines, but some other good stuff too.

We did reconnaissance training in which we observed a target for two days, devised a plan, hit the target, took simulated casualties, evacuated the casualties, pulled back to the point of origin and did the whole thing again. And again. Collectively, these drills are known as fuck-fuck games. We played many such games in Arkansas.

On weekends, after a morning shoot, the beer lamp was lit, and stayed lit until late Sunday. I'm not a big drinker, but some other guys in the platoon were. I don't know where they found the energy to drink to such excess after a grueling week of training, but that's what happened. G-unit and I always found time to get in a good workout instead.

The first Saturday of Land Warfare, the new guys were told to go to their rooms at noon and wait. While I was in my barracks room, a two story motel-style housing quarters, I could hear a group of old guys going door to door, rounding up the newbies and bringing them down stairs to the first level, one by one. Every once in a while I would hear a buzzing sound followed sharply by a yelp. *What the fuck are they doing?* I thought. Then came my turn.

Five old guys busted into my room, snatched me up like I was a high-value target and brought me downstairs, threw me in a chair and duct taped my hands behind my back. I was to stand trial in their kangaroo court.

"Carl, why the fuck were you late to formation Wednesday?"

"I wasn't late..."

Zzzzaapp!

"Oowww! What the fuck, dude?!"

Once they'd tazed me, I realized what had been the cause of the buzzing and yelping I'd heard earlier. The metal chair I was taped to snapped as my muscles seized from the shock.

"And Thursday you were in desert cammies, you were supposed to wear woodlands!"

Here it comes again, I thought.

Zzaapp!

"Aaahhggg! Fuck!"

They put my feet in a bucket of ice water, sprayed me down with a hose, threw flour on my head and body and hot sauce in my eyes, put a dead fish in my mouth and hurled eggs at my nuts. It was a team building exercise I guess.

"You're a good kid, Carl," Hog said. "Keep your shit together, you'll be alright."

We hugged it out after they cut me loose and they gave me a few beers to pound before Lenny was dragged in and I went back upstairs. After Land Warfare, we went back to headquarters to regroup for the next block of the work-up.

Dive Training

The word SEAL is an acronym for Sea, Air and Land combatant. In order to justify the Sea part of our title, we have to remain dive qualified, which is an absurd stipulation, because the last major dive op was Panama, 1989. Additionally, there are units called SEAL Delivery Vehicles or SDVs, whose job it is to do the underwater stuff. But most of us didn't go through Hell Week because we wanted to do that. We joined the Teams to jump out of airplanes and shoot bad guys in the face. But orders were orders, and we could tolerate sixty hours of dive time a year.

The water in Little Creek was murky, so visibility was minimal. It was a cesspool—an underwater gauntlet of debris, which had been accumulating since the 1950s. We set underwater mock charges, disarmed them, then set more. Most of us, including the older guys, hadn't been in the water with fins since SQT. A few guys got caught on snags underwater and developed infections. Nothing serious, but they wound up missing a few days of training which is generally frowned upon. I was one of them.

I developed an ear infection early on, but didn't say anything. On the fifth day of diving I was twenty-five feet down when I felt a pop in my head. I learned later that I had perforated my ear drum. When I came up, I noticed there was some yellow fluid coming out my left ear, but no blood, so I only missed a few days.

The intensity of SEAL training conditions you to ignore your body's warning signs; to endure severe cold and muscle fatigue and to tolerate extreme discomfort. In this context, it's easy to let something like ear pain turn into a significant injury by refusing to lay off, and instead trying to push through the pain. It's a balancing act: when to persevere and when to take injuries seriously.

The Dive Training block was sort of a joke. The worst part about it was that we were training to deploy to the Arabian Desert, and here we were swimming around Little Creek doing all this underwater demolition bullshit. It was a waste of time and resources.

Mobility Training

The next stop was Nevada for Mobility Training. We drove around in 998 Humvees—the ones that aren't up-armored—pushing the vehicles to their absolute limits on the off road driving course. Uneven terrain, sloping hills and valleys with a red rock dust surface closer to the likeness of

Afghanistan than Iraq. One time Rico was driving and I was up in the turret and he went forward off a small cliff and I slammed into the receiver of the .50 cal, nearly tumbling out of the turret. If it wasn't one thing with that guy, it was another.

We'd do long range convoys with live fire exercises, 300 miles out, bivouac in the high desert, than turn around and drive back. But we mostly worked on IADs. We would execute standard patrols and simulate taking contact, just as we had at land warfare. Only we were not on foot, we were in humvees. The humvees on the right would advance, engaging targets in excess of 500 meters some times, while the others would hang back and provide support fire. Then we would switch. Bounding overwatch with vehicles at speeds of thirty to fifty miles per hour on mountainous terrain, the wind whipping through our hair, the sound of automatic weapons fire like dynamite.

The challenge with this type of tactic was staying out of each others' line of fire. It was the responsibility of the gunners not to shoot any friendlies, but it was the drivers' responsibility not to encroach on another vehicle's sector of fire. This universal adherence to safety standards is a theme that permeates the culture of Naval Special Warfare. But even so, tempers flared.

On the drive back to base after a long day of off-roading and doing IADs, I noticed that Deuce and G-unit were in the middle of a shouting match, and this wasn't an ordinary shouting match. They were each in the turrets of their respective humvees, moving parallel to one another, traveling at fifty miles per hour on the road. I was up ahead, also in the turret, looking back at them, thinking, *What's going on with these two?*

They started throwing shell casings from spent .50 cal rounds at each other and saying things like, "I'm gonna fuck you up when we get back!"

I couldn't help but laugh. It was a serious, tense moment, but it was totally surreal. Here were these two elite warriors out in the middle of the Nevada Desert manning crew-served weapons, riding at speed down an interstate highway, huffing and puffing at each other like a couple of kids in a playground. You just don't see stuff like that everyday.

When we got back to base, G-unit was fuming. I'd never seen him like that. He went over to the staging area and started pacing, throwing punches into his hand, waiting for Deuce, who was shouting at him as Krom held him back. After a few minutes it became apparent they weren't going to actually fight, and Deuce was told to go to his room, which he did, giving G-unit a wide berth and conspicuously avoiding eye-contact.

After a few minutes G-unit started walking toward Deuce's room, in full beat-down mode. Thankfully Krom intercepted him, grabbed him lightly by the collar and told him to go to his room and cool off. Gonzales and I went with him.

"That motherfucker's been riding my ass since I got here!"

"Don't worry about Deuce," I said. "He's harmless."

"Man, fuck that motherfucker."

G-unit, at almost six feet tall, 230 lbs. and roughly six to eight percent body fat was a great fighter, (I'd seen him throw down in a bar fight one time) an awesome shot and a top-notch operator. There's no doubt he would have won in a scrap. Deuce was more bark than bite but could still throw down. G-unit was no bark, but he'd bite the shit out of you if you asked for it, and Deuce knew it. The situation defused itself, and we finished our training after a couple of weeks.

CQC

Close Quarter Combat training reinforced the most practically applicable skills we would employ on our deployment to Iraq. There was a range and two houses at the facility where we trained. In the mornings Echo was at the range and Foxtrot was at the first house. Then in the afternoons we'd switch. At night we'd hit both houses all together.

The range was for master level marksmanship. We spent so much time out there firing the rifle, reloading, firing the pistol, reloading, rifle to pistol transitions, pistol to rifle with a reload, stationary targets, pop-up targets, by the end, it was difficult to know where our appendages ended and our weapons began. A million jarring thunderclaps and the sweet stench of spent shell casings. After six hours we'd break for lunch, then hit the house.

The first house was like the Kill House back in Little Creek, but more elaborate, with more doors and better pop-up targets. If the range was for precision, the first house was for tactics. We did live breaches with charges and fired live rounds at the targets as we burned through the maze at full speed. At times, the cadre would switch us to sim rounds and put opposition against us. During one of those exercises, Rico shot me with a sim round.

"What the fuck, dude?"

"Uh, uh," He stuttered.

I shot him back and muttered, "Fuck you, asshole," under my breath just as the cadre stepped in to quell the confrontation.

At night Echo and Foxtrot platoons would come together for a night shoot in the second house. We all had Nods which amplified the ambient light, enabling us to see in the dark. Learning to operate effectively with Nods is extremely vital because ninety percent of our missions take place at night.

We got busy setting charges, breaching, clearing the first room, then the second, then on through to the end of the house. All clear, do it again. These were roughly thirteen to fourteen-hour training days. We were exhausted by the end, running on fumes, except for Krom who was powered by tobacco during training and whiskey while off the clock. I don't recall ever seeing him drink water, but somehow he was always at the top of his game. But we push so hard in training because in the fight, it's worse. We can be cut off for long periods of time or out on a recon for days. The suppression of fatigue is paramount.

After about a week, we started having competitions on the range; new guys vs. old guys.

The competitions were for speed. Two shooters stood parallel firing at two separate sets of six steel plates. The first shooter to drop all six was the winner. We newbies usually got our butts kicked, but G-unit actually outshot Rico, who'd been with the platoon for three years.

I bet Krom 500 push-ups I could beat him. When the bell rang, he smoked me, dropping six plates to my four.I did five sets of a hundred push-ups on the spot, then had to get back on the gun, my arms shaking.

To date, each SEAL had had hundreds of thousands, if not millions of trigger pulls. *Anyone* who fires that many rounds consistently in so short a time is bound to improve dramatically. By the end of the block, we all had our shit together and there was little if any difference in accuracy between everyone in the platoon.

MOUT

Our next training block was a program for Military Operations in Urban Terrain, or MOUT. The basis of MOUT in the larger sense is derived from lessons learned in the Battle of Hue City, Republic of South Vietnam, 1968 and more recently from the Second Battle of Fallujah, Iraq, 2004. This is room clearing, but on a massive scale of multiple buildings. In order for MOUT training to be effective, there must be a mock city in which to drill. Ours was located somewhere in Kentucky and consisted of a one mile by half-mile urban center complete with stadium, a school, an office building and several apartment housing units. By the middle 2000s, nearly every combat unit was doing some type of MOUT training during their pre-deployment workup. But Naval Special Warfare (NSW) did things a little differently.

We would helo in and fast rope onto the roof of a target, hold cordon/overwatch till the last guy was off the bird, then move down to the door of the apartment unit. For soft entries, we'd kick in doors or use a battering ram. If the door is unlocked, that's a soft entry too. Hard entries are when we use explosive charges to blast through.

Once in, it was the same tactics we'd rehearsed at the Kill House, then later at the CQC course. Move fast, hit your corner, stay out of the doorway (of death), clear the room, regroup and prepare for the next breach.

The facilitators of the MOUT site were able to bring forty to sixty college-aged students, mostly males, out to the mock city to play insurgents in a simulated battle. Armed with the same Blue Barrel paint pellet guns that we also carried, their job was to resist and defend against our assaults. It was a lot of fun, for them and for us.

I noticed that many of them wouldn't go down once they'd been hit (like they were supposed to). So the next day, I went to the Home Depot out in town and procured the makings of a potato cannon: some valves and a few feet of PVC pipe. When I got back to base I connected the cannon with a compressor from one of our humvees, which served as the compression mechanism. Instead of potatoes we used wet towels duct taped into cubes, stuffed down the bore of the cannon with a pool cue. The potato cannon was our heavy weapon. When we hit an "insurgent," he went down like a sac of potatoes. G-unit was a rockstar with that thing.

By the end of MOUT, we new guys had fully integrated into the platoon and were as ready as we'd ever be for war.

Comms School

When we got back to Little Creek, Beads and I were sent to a basic comms school to learn the fundamentals of electronic communications. They taught us how to load crypto, program frequencies, build antennas, and maintain the radio equipment; even how to turn an AM/FM car radio into one that can also transmit. It was a five-week course, the final week of which was spent outdoors field testing different radio systems and trouble shooting equipment malfunctions. I learned a lot.

JTAC

I must have done something to impress the Task Unit leadership because they sent me back out to Nevada, this time to attend Joint Tactical Air Controller school, a vital qualification to have in the career of any SEAL lucky enough to get it. I was the only one from Echo Platoon; there was one other guy there from Team 10. The purpose of this school was to teach us the protocol of communicating with aircraft: how to call for fire and MEDEVACs, how to deconflict artillery into restricted airspace and how to work with other services' artillery and air assets, including drones. I had gone through many training evolutions, but this one was advanced in a way I'd never before experienced. It was a major responsibility to be tasked with putting anything from a 2,000-pound bomb to supersonic strafing runs in close proximity to your teammates.

We learned how to warn friendly aircraft to stay clear of certain sectors of airspace because an artillery barrage would be coming through shortly. Or how to tell artillery emplacements, including Navy gunships, to adjust their fire for our friendlies in the sky. There were so many moving parts. This was not a simple assault. It was a sophisticated, coordinated effort to strike an enemy target without causing a friendly fire incident. Upon completion of the course, I was one of two guys from the platoon to be JTAC qualified.

SITEX

All of our individual training blocks culminated with SITEX. It was a two-week field op that was as close to a deployment as it gets. The entire Team, all three Task Units were out there at the same time executing complex missions. And there were Army guys and Marines in the battle space, too.

We'd hike into a mock city, hit a target, clear a few houses and simulate a capture. Then we'd call for extract, but when the bird got there, we'd receive "intel" about a follow-on target twenty miles away at another mock city. So, we'd helo in, fast rope onto a building, find the entrance and start breaching. Then we'd head back to base and break down the op. What did we do well, what did we screw up? Then we'd do it again.

It went on like that for a week. Full mission profile, sniper overwatch, vehicle interdictions, recon, the whole enchilada. All assaults executed at a grueling operational tempo. All I could think about was getting out there and doing it for real.

Before our ship date, we all took leave and did our own thing. I went home to Greenwich and spent time with Kaitlyn, the woman who would become my wife. We had gone to high school together, but hadn't started dating until a couple of years after graduation. But I knew she was the one for me. I'd bought a ring, and told her if she could make it through a deployment, I would propose. I knew how difficult things were for military spouses, especially in the Spec War community. I loved her, but I wanted to make sure she knew what she was in for.

One night, Kaitlyn and I, along with her whole family and some friends, went out to a local night club in neighboring Stamford. We were dancing, drinking, having a good time. Some drunk asshole tried making a pass at my soon-to-be sister in law. When she rebuffed his overtures, he threw a bottle across the bar and a small scuffle broke out, which was quickly de-escalated. The bouncers in the place wanted to know, "Who the fuck threw that bottle?"

The guy was sneaking out the door when Kaitlyn ran up to him and pointed.

"That's him, that's him!"

He turned around and punched her in the face, and I saw red. I literally reacted like it was an IAD. Of all the women in the place, this idiot assaults the fiancé of a SEAL days before he's slated to ship out to war. He and anyone in-between were in a world of shit.

Ordinarily, I don't fight. I realized when I was wrestling at Sacred Heart that I could really hurt people, so now, at 240 pounds, I made sure never to lose my temper. But this dude struck my woman, and that was unacceptable.

I got ahold of him and pounded his face in while the five or six bouncers tried to intervene. The guy knew right away he'd fucked up, but it was too late. Some of his friends tried to break it up, and they got some, too. I took some blows to the face and head, but kept on throwing punches. Kaitlyn's brother beat the shit out of three or four of them, too. Eventually, we were subdued by several bouncers and taken into police custody.

I explained to the desk sergeant what had happened and that I was a SEAL heading out to Iraq in a few days. He called down to Little Creek and got ahold of Krom, who verified that I was who I said I was, and they cut me loose. Unfortunately, my soon-to-be brother in law didn't have the same luck.

"Hey Carl," the desk sergeant said as I was walking out.

"Yes, sir?"

"Thank you for your service."

I spent time with my parents and sisters before I left, too. Far from the dysfunctional youth I once was, I had become a man; a warrior. And they were proud of me, but I could tell they were terrified. Especially my mom. She did her best to keep it cool, but I knew she was struggling.

"You be safe out there, bud."

"I will, Mom."

In the morning, I drove back to Virginia Beach. The following day we gathered at Team 10 Headquarters, where Beads and I had checked in a year and a half earlier with the Petty officer of the Watch screaming "Cyclops!" demanding that we jump into the surf in our dress blues. Training was over. It was time to punch in for real.

"All the guys going to Iraq, come over here a second," Boats said.

He'd replaced Hog during the work-up as Chief of Task Unit 3. He was now headed to Europe and Africa to train with our NATO allies along with the majority of Task Unit 3 — the guys I'd just spent the last year and a half doing the work-up with.

"Hey, y'all are about to see some shit," he went on. "Iraq is hot right now. Shoot straight, keep your fucking heads down when you're supposed to, listen to Bizzle and you'll all come home alive."

"Yes, Chief."

"Got it, Chief."

Bizzle had flown out a few weeks earlier with the advance party. From what I'd come to know of him, he was a real badass.

I got on the shuttle bus to the tarmac in civilian clothes, humping a rucksack full of uniforms, hygiene gear, a laptop, some personal effects and a hammock. The C-17 cargo aircraft were on standby when I walked up.

The Task Unit 3 guys who were headed to Europe loaded up and took off before we did, but it wasn't long before our C-17 pulled up and we had our gear—twenty or so 8'X8'X8' conex boxes full of weapons, armor, and all that stuff—loaded on and then walked up the ramp into the plane's massive mechanical belly. Shortly after, we were wheels up, headed to Baghdad. I pulled the hammock out of my rucksack, suspended it between two conex boxes and, with the help of an Ambien, crashed out for a few hours.

IRAQ - 1ST DEPLOYMENT

After a short refueling stop in Rammestein, Germany we were wheels up once more and in a few short hours our C-17 would touch down at Baghdad International Airport, at the time, one of the largest overseas US military installations in the world.

We had to land at night in order to avoid being shot out of the sky by a Rocket Propelled Grenade or other small arms fire during the approach. The pilot came over the intercom to tell us we were "going dark." The lights cut out and the air crewmen moved around the cargo area, making sure everything was secured before putting on their kevlar helmets and vests.

"How come they don't have to put their gear on?" I heard one air crewman ask another.

"They're SEALs," the other replied.

Stack met us at the airfield as we deplaned, exhausted from our long trip. "Hey guys, welcome to Baghdad."

In the short time it had taken us to unload our personal gear, I noticed the air crewmen had brought out our conex boxes and loaded up other cargo and taxied to another part of the air field for takeoff, all with their lights off. It dawned on me that we were within mortar range of the enemy, and the aircraft taxied around in the dark to avoid creating a target for insurgents; a small but poignant indicator that this new environment required adaptable responses to issues of security.

"Why don't you get set up in the trailers, then come over to the TOC in an hour?" Stack said.

"Roger that."

We were led to the double wide trailers by a skinny non-SEAL Navy admin guy.

"Welcome to the Hotel del Baghdad."

"Thanks."

The Sea Bees, Navy Construction Battalion builders and engineers, had made their way back to camp with the flatbed trucks and were transferring our conex boxes from the tarmac where the air crewmen had left them.

When I got to my room I noticed a familiar face.

"T-Mo, what's up man?"

"Hey, Carl, come on in. Make yourself at home."

T-Mo was from Foxtrot, our sister platoon in Task Unit 3. Most of the guys in Baghdad at that point were from Task Unit 2, but T-Mo and Bizzle, myself, and a few others were lucky enough to have been augmented.

I dropped my rucksack, laid down on my cot and closed my eyes a minute. I was unbearably fatigued, but I wouldn't allow myself to fall asleep. About a half hour later, I got up and walked over to the TOC. On the way there, I saw a few of the guys from the flight. They looked as run down as I felt.

"Alright, for some of you this is your first deployment. For some of you, it's business as usual," Stack addressed the roomful of new arrivals. "This is how things work," he went on. "We have a meeting every day at 1800 to go over our potential ops. We have three stages of ready. At the 1800 brief, we're on Green, which means there is no mission planned. Orange means standby—we got something but the details are still being ironed out. There are three places you can be when we're Orange: the gym, your rooms, or here in the TOC. When we're Red, you have fifteen minutes till we roll out. This means keep your shit ready at all times. When you get back from an op, before you wash your ass, re-jock your gear. We could get a call to Red anytime.

"Before we go out, we hit the ready room and load up, do last minute gear and comms checks and make sure we're not fucked up. We mostly do night ops, no daytime patrol bullshit like the Army. I know you're all tired; try to stay up through the night and go to sleep tomorrow morning so your schedule is right. We'll leave you off the roster tonight while you get adjusted. That's all."

"Thanks, Stack."

"Roger that, Stack."

"Good to go, Stack."

I went to the chow hall for a cup of coffee to keep myself wired through the night, then reluctantly hit the gym. When the following morning finally came, I crashed out on my cot and experienced some of the best sleep of my life.

The next two days were a relative blur. In my room in the trailers, I lofted my cot to create more space, and put a desk underneath the loft. I duct-taped the windows to keep the sunlight out so I could sleep better during the days, and I hit the gym at night to keep myself awake.

Guys I knew from training or from Team 10 like Doc Franky, Turtle, Drop, or Doc Jump were in-country, too, and I would see them in and around the camp. And Bizzle took the new guys under his wing, fielding the many naive questions we'd bother him with. The next night I popped into his room.

"Carl, what's up, man?"

"Hey, Bizzle. Just trying to get my sleep schedule sorted out. Any word on ops?"

"Nothing yet. I'm gonna hit the gym, see you over there. And don't get too comfortable, you're on the roster tonight."

"Roger that."

Bizzle was well respected at the Teams. He'd deployed far and wide to places I'm not allowed to mention. I knew he maintained a high level of excellence and demanded the absolute best of his SEALs. He almost never gave praise, because he expected perfection. To not get your ass chewed by him was considered praise. A few hours later, after a smash session at the gym, he dropped by my room.

"Sack up, baby. We're Orange!"

"Good to go."

My head was swimming; this was finally it. Three years of pushing my mind and body to their absolute limit all for this moment: my first mission. I went to my room and changed into desert cammies. We took care to leave the name plates and patches off our uniforms.

Since we were Orange, I had to stay close to the TOC. It was an impossible feeling, knowing that we'd be heading out soon, but still having to wait around for the order. It was the *hurry up and wait* feeling.

"You ready, Carl?"

"Fuck yeah, I'm ready!"

I was visibly fired up, but also nervous.

"Don't get too amped before we head out. You'll have nothing left for the fight."

J. Louie had been around for a while. He was a SEAL with advanced intelligence and reconnaissance training and a special clearance that allowed him to work with the Other

Government Agencies (OGAs). He hung around with Steve, a non-SEAL Navy Intel guy.

"I can't stand this waiting around bullshit," I said.

"Calm down," J. Louie replied. "This is the first of many. We'll be out there in a minute."

Word was passed that we were Red, so T-Mo and I made for the ready room to load up on mags and do last minute checks. Our interpreter for this op was the infamous Johnny Walker. He'd been working with the SEALs since the invasion in '03 and was a well known figure in and around the Teams.

"Heeeeerrrrreee's Johnny!" Stack hollered across the open air outside the ready room.

"Stack, my man! Here we go again, are you ready for the shit?" Johnny asked.

A minute later we were at the trucks briefing the details of the op on the fly over comms.

"Holy shit, look at this yard sale!" J. Louie shouted at Dan, referring to his display of extra gear; knee pads, elbow pads, shoulder pads, etc. "You look like a fucking Teenage Mutant Ninja Turtle, man."

He would henceforth be known as Turtle.

Ours was the third vehicle in a convoy of six and I was driving. The base was so huge that it took us nearly half an hour to clear the front gate.

Once we crossed the threshold, we all killed our headlights and fired up our Nods, moving like ghosts at seventy miles per hour northeast through Baghdad toward Sadr City. We made sure to take back roads to avoid being hit by an IED.

When we arrived at the target area, we used the vehicles to cordon off an entire city block. There were several houses that we were to hit simultaneously, and we didn't want any squirters—enemy combatants who flee out the backdoor as we're kicking in the front—to get away. Turtle was in the turret behind the .50 Cal. I was outside the truck, watching and waiting.

The most vulnerable time for a capture team during a mission is either when they're breaching the door, or when they've got the guys hooded and flexicuffed and they're bringing them back to the trucks. This is because the whole neighborhood will have seen them go in, and could, ostensibly, be setting up on them for when they come out. For this reason, it's customary for the capture team to radio up to the guys on cordon that the target is secured and they're about to haul ass back to the trucks, and that's exactly what happened.

"Target secure, we're coming out now!"

"Roger that!"

The capture team thundered out to the humvees with three individuals bound and hooded. My head was on a swivel scanning for enemy activity until the last possible second when everyone piled inside and I got behind the wheel and we were off, seventy miles per hour back across Baghdad to the airport.

We had a small detention facility next to the OGA hut in our compound that we brought prisoners to first before turning them over to the garrison higher ups. We did this because we wanted our guys, Bobby and J. Louie, to have the first opportunity to interrogate potential sources.

Once the guys were done interrogating the prisoners, they radioed over to the main side of the base for a transfer and these Navy Masters at Arms (military police) showed up and took custody of the prisoners with their chests puffed out like they were the ones who actually brought them in. It always made me laugh out loud when they did this, which was often.

After that first mission, we started opping every night. The tempo was unreal. We'd get the brief at 1800. Eat, hit the gym, dick around for a few hours, hit the ready room and load up, then roll out. Every mission we did was capture/kill. Our primary objective was to locate high-value individuals, apprehend them, bring them back to base and turn them over to our Intel guys. If we, for whatever reason, were unable to take them alive, we had the legal authority to kill them, which we often did when they left us no other option.

In addition to our operational duties, we also were tasked with training the Iraqi Special Forces, an outfit whose professionalism left much to be desired. They were constantly late for training; sometimes they wouldn't bother showing up. Our interpreters (terps) — Johnny Walker or Axe — would communicate to them what we wanted them to do, but a lot of times, it wouldn't resonate. This one soldier kept leaving his index finger inside the trigger guard of his AK while he dangled it in his right hand, barrel facing the ground like it was a pistol. We told him several times not to hold the weapon like that and to keep his finger off the trigger until he was ready to fire. He ignored us, and eventually the weight of the rifle pressing down on his trigger finger caused the weapon to go off right next to his foot, causing shrapnel to pepper his foot and leg. Once we determined the wound was not life-threatening, we all chuckled as we called over the medic. One less moron to worry about, we all thought.

Also, we always brought them to the firing range on our compound, never to our berthing area or chow hall. And oddly enough, when we got hit with mortars, they struck in exactly the place where we'd held training with the Iraqis; never anywhere else. It was widely speculated that the Iraqis had done pace counts from the main gate or taken GPS coordinates and relayed the information to enemy fighters, or simply fired on us themselves, but we were never able to prove it.

The first two weeks, all of our capture missions went off without a hitch; not a single shot was fired. *This can't last*, I remember thinking.

"Wait till it gets warmer," Stack said. "They like to fight more in the late Spring."

We'd blown past a few IEDs on the road that detonated after our trucks had cleared the kill zone, and luckily no one had yet been hurt. But our buttholes puckered. We tried to stay off Route Michigan—AKA IED Alley—as much as we could, but sometimes it was the only way we could go.

One night while we were on target, holding cordon with the humvees, a few locals tried to get in close to see what was going on. They knew we wouldn't shoot civilians like Saddam's troops would have (and did), so they weren't intimidated at all by our rifles. I shoved one back and told him to fuck off, and the rest followed suit. A few minutes later a squirter shot out of the target building and one of the other guys tackled him.

After about two weeks of this pace, me and a few other guys walked over to Bizzle's trailer to see if our tempo was normal, or if we were going to slow it down anytime soon.

"I'm barely getting a few hours sleep before we have to muster at the TOC. I'm totally fried."

"You're fucking Navy SEALs in Iraq. You know how many guys would kill to trade places with you? Get the fuck over it." We could tell that Bizzle was just as tired as us, but he towed the line.

We were out on cordon one night a week or so later when I noticed a guy creeping around on the roof of the target building. The capture team had gone in, and I was at the truck waiting with Turtle. I had my Nods on, but still couldn't tell if he was carrying a weapon, so I radioed to the eye in the sky.

"Two-Zero, this is Zero-Five, over."

The protocol for military radio transmissions is to say the name of the call sign you're trying to reach first, then identify yourself next.

"Go ahead Zero-Five."

"I'm marked by IR strobe, corner of Mike and Blue (our predetermined names for roads that night.) I have movement, top of the building seventy-five meters north my position. Can you get a visual, over?"

"We see him. We can't confirm he has a weapon, over."

"Roger that. Keep a sensor on him if you can."

A few minutes later I heard a salvo of snap-pops just above my head and I dropped down behind the vehicle to take cover. A round impacted a wall a few feet behind me.

"Two-Zero, Zero-Five. Contact from rooftop. Say when ready for 5-line, over."

"Zero-Five, Two-Zero. Send it."

I relayed the 5-line (which I had practiced over a thousand times in training) to the air asset then radioed the capture team to let them know there was about to be a loud boom, and that it was coming from our side. All the while that asshole on the roof continued to take pot shots at us.

"Zero-One, Zero-Five, be advised: I've called for fire on the roof of the building, over."

"Zero-Five, that's a good copy. Thanks for the heads up, we'll be out in a minute."

There were a few more shots from the roof, then the munitions hit, and with a fierce explosion and a flash of white light from the sparks, the pot shots stopped.

"Zero-Five, Two-Zero: target is neutralized."

"Thanks for the help, gents."

"No problem. Two-Zero, out."

The assault team radioed that they'd got the guy and were headed back to the trucks and that we'd better have our shit together, and I said, "Roger that."

They hauled ass with the prisoner in tow, loaded him into one of the humvees and we were off, tearing ass through Baghdad back to base, where we would turn over our charge to the Intel guys, then finally to the Masters at Arms who would pump their chests out when they took custody of him. We then rode back to main side.

"Hey Carl," Bizzle halled me over the radio.

"Yeah?"

"Good job back there."

"Thanks, Bizzle."

One night after a run-of-the-mill capture mission, we returned to base, delivered our prisoners and turned in. We attended our regular brief and shortly after dark we were wheels up, on our way to another objective. We hit the target taking contact. As we were egressing, I observed that the insurgents had set fire to the block of homes we'd just engaged.

"What the fuck is going on?" I said out loud to no one in particular.

I was getting in the back of the humvee with Bizzle and Axe. We were in the flat bed of the truck's back end, exposed and vulnerable. Most US forces, Marines and Army, had only one shooter per humvee—the guy in the turret. But we had four, myself, two others in the back, and Turtle in the turret. This went for every vehicle in the convoy as well. In order to make our weapons effective we had to put ourselves outside the protective armor of the humvee, so we rode on the vehicle's back end like a couple of kids in the bed of a pick-up truck.

On the way out, our commanding officer, Bob, came over the SATCOM and told us to hit the same target we'd hit the night before.

"Sir, I don't think that's a good idea," Stack radioed back.

"That's the way it is," Bob answered.

It was a few minutes drive back to the target and we took it without incident, conducting a cordon-search and loading back up to get the fuck out of Sadr City.

We were second to last in the marching order. Peg was driving the rear vehicle, with Doc Jump in the turret, J. Louie, Steven, and Bobby in the backseat with one of our terps. Rooster, the convoy's Tactical Commander (TC) was in the backseat.

The convoy rounded a sharp righthand turn, when I heard the loudest explosion I'd ever heard. I'm not sure if I lost consciousness or not, but I remember firing at muzzle flashes, engaging as best I could with my vision blurred.

"What the fuck?!"

The explosion had just missed our humvee, but had struck a direct hit on the rear vehicle, which, miraculously, was still moving forward. I saw smoke coming from the damaged humvee as it swerved side to side along the road. Bizzle and I knew then that the situation was serious.

Jump crawled down from the nearly destroyed turret, where the .50 caliber machine gun barrel had been sheered clean off, to render aid to the wounded.

"Peg, talk to me buddy!" Rooster hollered over the radio. "Are you alright? What's the damage?"

"I'm hit in the fucking leg but I'm good. Jump is in the back working on them, standby."

"Can you keep going?"

"I'm good, just get us the fuck out of here!"

"Roger that." Rooster radioed headquarters. "TOC, this is C2. We've been hit by an IED, some guys in bad shape. Three, maybe four. We're east of Sadr City, Find us a fucking FOB with a landing zone, we need a MEDEVAC, over." Before the TOC could even get back to us our lead navigator, Nick Cheque, had plotted the course

"Roger that. There's an Army FOB two klicks from your location. Keep going straight, it'll be on your left. Look out for the constantina wire. I'll let them know you're headed there now. We'll get a MEDEVAC out to you immediately. Let us know when you've arrived, over."

"Roger that." Rooster changed gears and began directing our response. "Victor 5, switch places with 6."

"Got it."

Stack came over the radio and confirmed our fears. "J. Louie and Steve, KIA. Bobby's got a pulse, but it's weak."

Those words will echo in my mind forever, even as I write them here. I am humbled by those men; better men than me. We weren't out of Dodge yet. We dropped back to the rear position because the vehicle that sustained the blast had lost the ability to return fire, and also in case Peg lost consciousness, we could use our humvee to push his truck.

But he managed to stay alert and drive the blown out humvee through the serpentine of dirt filled hesco barriers into the Army FOB.

The Army guys didn't know what to make of us. We came barreling through their Entry Control Point and began unloading our casualties, while they just stared, dumbstruck for a moment. But after the initial shock, they snapped out of it and helped us parse the mass casualty situation.

I was still a little woozy from having my bell rung earlier, but I shook it off and grabbed Bobby, our combat cameraman, out of the truck. He was unconscious, bleeding steadily with his Nods smashed into his face. I could see skeletal damage under the skin, so I set him down and Jump came by and continued to treat his injuries, which included major trauma to both orbital cavities.

Stack grabbed J. Louie, who had been killed instantly when the humvee was hit, and brought him over to a spot on the ground away from the trucks. After he'd directed the mass casualty response, Stack knelt down beside his longtime friend and shed the toughest tear of his life. He'd known J. Louie for fifteen years. They'd grown up together in the Teams. I'd never seen that emotional side of him before. Everyone gave him space.

Steven, our non-SEAL Navy Intel guy had also been killed, and Mohammed, our interpreter had suffered a mild traumatic brain injury without a visible scratch on him. We

MEDEVACed out Peg and Bobby as soon as the birds could land.

Jump had dressed the hole in Peg's leg, which had been caused by a piece of shrapnel, with gauze and secured it with an ace wrap. He then stuck him with an IV of Hextend, a solution designed to draw fluid from the interstitial space between layers of skin and funnel it into blood vessels to compensate for blood loss.

The closest helicopters were two Apache gunships and two MH-5s, one of which stayed hovering overhead while the other touched down in the tiny landing zone. Because the Apaches were attack helicopters and not troop carriers, the only seats they had were for the pilot and copilot in their respective cockpits. But the copilot was mission-centric; he grabbed Peg and helped him into his seat in the rear cockpit, and in a flash, they were gone, en route to the trauma center at Camp Victory in Baghdad where a team of surgeons would try in vain to keep Peg's leg from being amputated in the long run due to nerve damage. (The military doctors accidentally left a golf ball-sized piece of copper from the IED projectile in his leg, which caused the nerve to die, ultimately leading to the amputation below the knee of his leg years later.)

We sent our KIAs—Steven and J. Louie—with small helicopters about twenty minutes after Peg had been MEDEVACed. Since there was no room inside, we strapped them to spine boards and bound them to the loading deck over the twin mini-guns on either side. We all watched as they were hoisted into the sky, disappearing into the desert night as the rumble of the rotor blades softened to a dull roar, eventually fading out of earshot. We looked at each other. *What was there to say?* It was the first time I'd lost friends in combat. It was a sobering moment. I realized that it would be several months before I was out of there, so I had to keep my head in the game. We all did.

REDEPLOYMENT

"Grab your shit, let's go," Bizzle said.

"Roger that."

I policed up all my gear from the room at the trailers (which wasn't much to begin with), and hauled it over to the C-17 transport plane which lay idling on the tarmac with its loading ramp down.

"Hey, Carl," Bizzle called to me as I walked into the plane.

"Yeah?"

"Good work. See you back at Little Creek."

"See you back there, man. Be safe."

Pinky, one of the JTACs from Echo Platoon that had been deployed to Germany, had to cut his tour short for personal reasons, so I was being flown in to replace him until Team

10 rotated back to Little Creek at the end of October. It was a smooth ride, and I had the entire cabin to myself. I even played frisbee with some of the air crewmen once we'd cleared hostile airspace.

When I landed in Germany I was met at the airfield by one of the support guys who got behind the wheel for the forty-five minute drive back to Stuttgart where our base was. It was odd seeing so much greenery after months of nothing but desert sand and the odd palm tree. Also, I had to adjust to the Western European time zone and to being awake during the day again, and asleep (hopefully) at night. Five-plus months of opping on vampire time had taken its toll.

Everyone from Echo and Foxtrot wanted to hear about Iraq so, over beers, I told them about what we'd seen, what we'd done, and what I'd learned. They all seemed to understand.

For the rest of the deployment we trained with the Germans, the Lithuanians, the Romanians and even the Azerbaijanis, doing mostly air ops and dive training but also live fire drills and infantry tactics, too. It was fun and interesting, but nothing like combat. I quickly realized the things that used to get my blood pumping — sky diving, and driving really fast — no longer did it for me.

About a month into my time in Europe we received new check-ins fresh out of SQT. It was a little unusual to have guys join the Team mid-deployment, but not unheard of. I met Echo Platoon's new-new guys, McCabe, Nelson, and Ace at the airport in Munich.

It was funny to gauge the reactions of bystanders as these three clean-cut, very fit young guys toted a rolling cart stacked with military gear and gun cases through the civilian airport in the middle of the day.

I was in a weird limbo stage of my service because, technically, I was still a new guy since we hadn't officially finished the deployment cycle, even though I'd already seen more shit than half the people in the Teams. But I was senior to these new knuckleheads, so I had to set a good example if I expected them to be good SEALs in turn. And they were good.

After the series of training trips, while everyone else headed back to the states, McCabe and I flew to TQ, an airbase in Iraq, to avoid a tax penalty on our reenlistment bonuses. I was happy to give the Teams six more years; this was my dream job.

When we got back to Little Creek, everyone spread out and took leave. I hung out with Kaitlyn. Because I didn't leave town, I kept getting called into work during my leave days to supervise this or that. I didn't have enough rank to tell the duty officer to piss off, so I sucked it up. This was protocol. If the duty desk knew you were local when you took some days off, it was not unusual to get called in for "just a few minutes," which invariably meant at least half the day. But I couldn't really complain because half the time we took leave, we weren't charged the days.

When everyone had gotten back from leave, the story swapping began in earnest. From the general consensus, Germany was a booze fest, Africa sucked, and Iraq was a war zone.

At an awards ceremony where all of Team 10 (ninety-six SEALs and about twice that number in support staff) was present, Stack and Rooster both got Bronze Stars with the letter V on top of the ribbon to denote "Valor." It wasn't the first Bronze Star for either of them. I got a Joint Service Commendation Medal, also with a V. In fact, nearly all the awards given to operators had Vs on them. I can remember seeing the faces of the new guys as the awards were being read aloud at the ceremony: *Engaged multiple enemy targets with little regard for his own life, responsible for X-thousands of pounds of air to ground munitions...responsible for multiple enemies killed...led to capturing multiple high-value targets,* etc.

It was good to be back in Echo Platoon with some of the guys I'd done the work-up with like Krom, Lenny, and G-Unit. Deuce had been transferred to Task Unit 1 and was shot several times on the subsequent deployment, but survived his injuries, eventually making almost a full recovery, thank God, they even gave him the silver star.

We also had a lot of new check-ins. Among them was Keefe. I looked out for him and McCabe just as Krom had looked out for me. One day we were sitting in a break room at Task Unit 3 when Jimmy, our new platoon OIC, came in and said, "Hey, guys."

"Hey, LT," we all replied in unison.

"Carl, have these guys been to the kill house?"

"Not yet."

"Take them."

"Roger that."

G-unit, Gonzales, and I took Keefe and McCabe to the armory to draw Blue Barrels before bringing them to the kill house.

"Listen up, guys," Gonzales said. "These weapons don't fire real rounds, but you need to treat them like they do. Alright?"

"Good to go."

"Roger that."

We breached the first door and cleared each room, blowing through the house in under two minutes.

"Faster!" called a voice from the rafters. It belonged to Jimmy, our new OIC. He was up there with Tweak, a roided out LPO who earned his nickname through numerous displays of erratic behavior. They sat up there chiding and directing us all afternoon as we cleared and re-cleared that house, breaking down what worked and what didn't in discussions between raids. Keefe and McCabe were rough around the edges, but had the makings of great SEALs, and I was glad they had come to Echo.

In the years since I had graduated BUD/S, the leadership in Coronado began relaxing standards and requirements in an effort to push more SEALs through to the Teams; guys who would have otherwise quit or washed out. One of the things they did was get rid of winter classes. The air temperature is dramatically lower in the winter months, as is the ocean water. I know this intimately because I graduated from a winter class. How a person responds to the freezing, wet, chafing conditions of Coronado is what determines whether or not he is mentally fit for service with the Teams. A lot of guys got through that shouldn't have, but Keefe and McCabe were the real thing and we were lucky to have them.

Finally, after four-plus years in the Navy, the majority of which was spent either training or on deployment, I was no longer a Fucking New Guy, or FNG. I was now a fire team leader (and soon to be squad leader) and the lead JTAC for Echo Platoon, SEAL Team 10. In accordance with my rise in status came an expansion of my duties and responsibilities. I was now a part of the planning element of all things platoon or mission related. This was a gut-check to me, because now, over and above how I conducted myself on an op, any mistakes I might make could potentially get people killed, especially as I would be the one directing 500-plus pound bombs coming out of the sky at supersonic speeds. The thought of this only motivated me further.

And the cycle continued. A few months after we'd all gotten back, we began the workup for the next deployment. We went to all the same training blocks as before with a new one added out in Indiana. It felt strange going through identical blocks of training with the same content as the previous work-up. Having seen actual combat, at this point, I had a much better grasp of why we did some of the things we did and was able to better apply my skills. It became apparent quickly, though, that some in our head shed didn't possess the same practical knowledge that my generation of SEALs had acquired early on in our careers as the result of having seen significant combat. Frequently, mine and other one-platooners' suggestions would be overruled by Tweak or Gibby. And often Training Detachment (TRADET), the command responsible for hosting and facilitating the training blocks, would side with us later on, during the debrief. This drove a wedge between ourselves and our platoon leadership, many of whom had not seen a great deal of combat.

In Indiana, the additional CQC and MOUT courses were set up in an abandoned hospital campus. There were multiple buildings and an adjoining courtyard, and different terrain features spanning a three-square-mile campus, so we were able to take full advantage of countless tactical scenarios requiring coordinated movement and communication.

Stack had left Team 10 and taken a command posting at TRADET. In his new role, he oversaw three of the training blocks we were going through, including the one in Indiana, which were universally regarded as the most difficult and pertinent to the modern battlefield. It's no wonder they chose Stack to run them.

"Carl, look at you! Fucking squad leader!"

"Well, they had to give it to somebody."

"Hahahaha. Who are these FNGs?"

"That's Keefe and McCabe."

"Hey, what's up, Stack?" McCabe said.

"Good to meet you, Stack." Keefe said.

Stack pointed to me and said, "Now you listen to this motherfucker, do what he tells you and you'll be okay."

He knew and I knew and perhaps Keefe and McCabe knew as well that the gods of war were indiscriminate. We could do everything right, not fuck up once and still get blown up or shot. I'd seen it happen firsthand. But the new guys have to know that we have their backs, that we wouldn't ever tell them to do something we wouldn't do ourselves. They have to trust us in order for this thing to work. And I trusted Stack, and Keefe and McCabe trusted me and for that I was grateful.

At Land Warfare we put all the new guys through the Kangaroo Court, but rather than taze them, we made them do sprints and other physical tasks. And we ran with them and made sure we beat them. Unit cohesion was paramount. I wanted those under me to be inspired to push harder than they ever had. And it worked. My generation of SEALs, especially those of us in Echo platoon, were bigger, faster, and stronger than any others Team 10 had ever seen, and we wanted it to be known to our new guys that they needed to be able to keep up.

We had two Explosive Ordinance Disposal (EOD) techs go through the workup with us: Grandpa (we called him this because, despite being just over thirty years old, his overall demeanor was that of someone collecting Social Security) and Tyler. They were SEALs in all but name. They hadn't gone through BUD/S but they were full-fledged members of the Naval Special Warfare community and they had our respect. Their job was to dispose of potentially dangerous explosive ordinance that might pose a threat to us. And let me tell you, they can have that job because they were often times running into the places that even we SEALs were running away from, to defeat the one enemy we didn't know how to fight: IEDs.

The role of EOD was greatly expanded in the post-9/11 War on Terror era because the enemy had discovered the effectiveness of IED strikes against coalition targets. And as their tactics evolved, so did our countermeasures, so between the bomb makers and EOD and mine sweepers there was a mini arms race all throughout the early and middle 2000s. Because unexploded ordinance was so dangerous, the default procedure for as long as I'd been with the Teams was to blow an IED in place. They were, generally speaking, way too dangerous to move.

There's a popular myth about EOD techs—no doubt thanks to Hollywood's gross misrepresentations—that their job is to disarm or defuse bombs. While they do receive extensive training on different types of explosives and how to neutralize them, mainly what EOD does is blow shit up. There's no red wire, blue wire nonsense. Not in the real world. It's too dangerous. The only way to effectively neutralize a bomb or IED without putting oneself at risk unnecessarily is to blow it up.

Grandpa was the senior tech. He'd done several platoons and was competent in the science of ordinance disposal. Tyler was the new guy, barely old enough to legally order a drink, full of vigor and curiosity. It was his first platoon, so he was eager to cut his teeth. But he was a goofball outside of working hours. We called him Mosquito because at the bar, he would conjoin five or six straws, creating a tiny syphon and come up behind people and suck their drinks down through the straws while they weren't looking. Everyone loved Mosquito; he was the platoon's little brother.

In between training blocks, Kaitlyn and I got married. It was a large wedding, almost sixty SEALs in attendance, plus friends and family. The night before, Jimmy and I reconned an island in the background of the ceremony site with a large water tower. Around 11 PM we swam over half a mile in the dark to the island through a busy shipping lane to put up a banner that read "Carl & Kaitlyn." Upon our return to shore, a few drunks on the beach noticed us coming out of the water in wetsuits, faces painted. One of them shouted, "What, you guys think you're some kinda Navy SEALs or something?"

I assumed it would be bad luck to bash their skulls in the night before my wedding, and Jimmy agreed, so we ignored them.

Kaitlyn and I tied the knot on a Saturday, I shipped out to Nevada for Mobility Training the following Monday. We would have to put off our honeymoon until my pre-deployment leave period.

One night Kaitlyn woke me up from a deep sleep.

"Can you tell those guys outside to keep it down?"

There'd been a party at a neighbor's house down the road earlier in the evening, and some stragglers had migrated over to my property and were making a ruckus.

"OK, I'll take care of it."

I peered out the back window that overlooked the back porch where the noise was coming from, and observed six men trying to get in through the back door. I turned to Kaitlyn and calmly said, "Call the cops, I'm going to go deal with this."

"Is everything alright?" she asked, concerned.

"Yeah, it's fine," I said in a reassuring tone.

Kaitlyn's mom, pregnant sister, brother-in-law and their three kids were visiting, so I was quiet going down the stairs because I didn't want to disturb them. When I got to the kitchen, I saw the guys in the backyard through the window. One of them was fiddling with the backdoor lock.

I moved tactically downstairs and stacked against the door with my Sig 239. In the event that they came in, I would be able to block their entry. I knew they couldn't see me through the window because it was dark in the house, so I had the element of surprise on my side. It would be only a matter of time before they got through, so I devised a plan to hit the fourth guy and divide the force. Most likely, the remaining two would take off, I thought. It didn't look like they were carrying weapons, but I wasn't taking any chances.

My hand was steady as I crouched next to the door. My combat experience and training made the experience as normal as putting shoes on. I had the upper hand for sure, and when it opened, my training and experience took over.

The first guy crept inside and moved across the kitchen in the direction of Kaitlyn's purse, which lay on the counter next to the sink. The next guy followed, then the next and I realized they were all pretty drunk. All I could think was, *you motherfuckers picked the wrong house to break into!*

As the fourth guy walked past me, I grabbed him by the collar with my left hand and struck the side of his head with the butt end of the pistol grip. He went down hard, and just as I'd thought they would, the remaining two guys took off. The guy that had been first in the house turned around and saw me standing there with the Sig in my hand and went white.

The other two came at me and I was able neutralized them quickly. The first guy then tried to go through me, but my knee to his face ended the assault. Of the four who entered the house, two ended up getting up and stumbling away while I detained the other two. I was just interested in making sure that they wouldn't get upstairs, so if they ran off, mission accomplished.

Once I had gotten them outside, I told them not to move until the police got there. I could have used lethal force, I would have been within my rights to do so, but my biggest concern was my nieces and nephews upstairs sleeping. I didn't want to wake them with gunfire and I didn't want them to see any dead bodies.

Kaitlyn came down to see what was going on and saw that I had everything under control. Miraculously, my in-laws slept through the whole thing! Forty minutes later, the first cop arrived, a young woman, maybe five-foot-three. She got out of the squad car and saw the two guys laid out on the grass and immediately drew her pistol.

"Police! Put your hands in the air!"

"Whoa, relax! This is my house, we're the ones that called you!"

I put my weapon down very slowly, raised my hands and after a moment of tension, she realized we were the good guys and the bad guys were face down on the grass. A few other squad cars arrived shortly after and my yard became a crime scene. Kaitlyn confirmed that no shots were fired, but they took my Sig anyway to run forensics on it.

Some other kids from the party made their way to my yard and started throwing red plastic cups at the squad cars. I thought there was going to be more trouble, but nothing happened. The next day I had to go down the police station to pick up my Sig and fill out some paperwork. Moral of the story: don't break into people's houses. You'll never know if the homeowner is a SEA.

The morning we flew out to Iraq, Kaitlyn drove me to the base.

"Crazy," she said.

"Yeah."

This time, however, she waited on base till the very last moment with all the other wives.

Teary-eyed, she looked up at me while I held her and said, "I'll see you soon, OK? I love you."

She buried her face in my chest, while I fought to hold back my own tears.

"I love you too, babe."

We loaded onto the bus and were off to the airport. The mood was somber. We were all wondering if we'd ever see our loved ones again. As we rolled up to the airport, we could see our C-17 pull up and drop its ramp as the Sea Bees began loading up our conex boxes.

Even though the airport was inside the boundary of Norfolk Naval Base, and we were high level operators, most with Top Secret security clearances on our way to Iraq to fight for our country, we still had to go through airport security like ordinary schlubs. The $10 an hour rent-a-cop at the gate corralled us into line to go through a metal detector. The look on his face when we told him that we were all packing was priceless. He froze up for a minute before phoning his supervisor, who arrived at the security checkpoint moments later. They tried to give us some lip about how we couldn't carry weapons through a military airport, but our senior officer wasn't having it. He pointed to the C-17 being loaded up by the Sea Bees and explained that inside the conex boxes were .50 caliber machine guns, mini guns, rockets, grenades, ammunition, plastic explosives, and a few hundred M-4 carbines, and that we were Navy SEALs on our way to Iraq. If we were packing Sig Sauer 9 mils, so what? If we were planning to do something terrible, we'd have done it already, and there would have been nothing he could have done to stop it. And with that, we shuffled past the dumbfounded rent-a-cop supervisor and got on the plane back to Iraq.

IRAQ - 2ND DEPLOYMENT

We flew into Al Taqaddum (TQ), an air base that serves Anbar Province, and convoyed out to Baharia, just outside Fallujah in the new RG-33 vehicles. The RGs were much larger than Humvees, significantly heavier and less maneuverable. But they had more armor and could withstand a much greater blast. They looked like up-armored beige fire engines. For all their IED resistant design work, I still preferred the faster, more agile 1114 up-armored humvees. In the period of time between my deployments, the war had experienced an evolution of technology and tactics, and from what I would soon learn, an updated Rules of Engagement policy.

All of Task Unit 3 had been deployed to Western Iraq, with a small detachment of fewer than ten SEALs from Echo

Platoon augmenting the base at Baharia. The remaining elements of TU3 were spread out among four different locations.

The compound at Baharia was pretty bare bones. We stayed in a cordoned off section of the much larger base called Camp Schwedler. Baharia, a once important, bustling base inside was in the process of being abandoned by US Forces as part of the drawdown. The base next door, Camp Fallujah, was almost completely empty by this point. Prior to that, under Saddam's regime, it served as a private vacation spot for his son, Uday. There were rumors that the lake on post doubled as a dumping ground for whores and servants who displeased the fickle prince.

Our small complex boasted a gym (of course), a chow hall, a TOC, housing trailers, an armory and a motor pool. And we almost never left. It was nothing like my first deployment. Our Team leadership didn't want to engage enemy targets. There had been a changing of the guard at the White House and it was clear that the new policy objective was to minimize the number of casualties on both sides. If there were no incidents, the President could claim victory and bring the troops home, which is what he promised to do during his campaign. The only problem with that is there were people in Fallujah, people we knew about—former Saddam-regime military officers, Baath

Party loyalists, and assorted militiamen—that are now, in all likelihood, key members of the ISIS leadership. We had the intelligence and the capability (but not the political will) to go after them back in 2009, and I know what I'm talking about because I was there. We did not win the war in Iraq, we left out of political convenience, and as a result, ISIS was able to take hold.

There were times we had reliable intel on the location of a known insurgent or Al Qaeda in Iraq operative and had to pass that intel on to an Army Special Forces or Marine unit because our leadership was too apprehensive to approve the mission. It went on like that for a while.

On our downtime (and there was a plethora of downtime) we were challenged to come up with new ways of passing the time. The gym was the most obvious solution, but even that became tiresome after a while. I built a thirty-foot-tall medieval trebuchet with wood planks, nuts, bolts, washers, and rope that could launch a projectile a few hundred feet. It probably could have gotten even more range, but the counterweight I used was a block of concrete and didn't generate enough force to hurl the projectile any further.

I also made a go-cart out of some spare engine parts and rode around the base at full speed, which wasn't very fast at all. Others turned to video games or watched endless amounts of TV.

Mosquito started going out on patrols with the Marines in the adjacent compound just to get some experience prosecuting IEDs. He wanted to work, that's why he was here, and the Marines were happy to have an EOD tech on convoy with them. Who wouldn't be?

I communicated with Kaitlyn via Skype or telephone every day or so. We were essentially newlyweds. I wanted to be near her. But I couldn't be, so Skype was as good as it got. The distance apart was a source of constant stress on a new relationship, on top of the fact that since the day we were married, some nine months earlier, we'd spent fewer than thirty days together due to the pre deployment work-up training schedule.

One day around mid-afternoon I heard a giant *kaboom* that seemed to come from just outside the wire. A few of us scrambled onto the roof to see if there were shots being fired so we could get in on the action.

Often, when a convoy is struck by an IED, the insurgents will launch a secondary ambush to maximize the number of casualties. When a vehicle is hit and disabled, the attackers will wait for troops to start evacuating their wounded before they strike again. We knew this, and remained vigilante.

Lenny, Gonzales and I climbed onto the roof of one of the buildings to get a better look.

We saw a huge cloud of black smoke rising from the end of a convoy that was stopped on the road about a mile outside the base, and wondered if we were going to have to suit up and leave the post. Had the vehicles been moving, I'd have figured that the strike was unsuccessful, but because they were stopped, we all knew something was wrong.

"Anyone seen Mosquito?" Jimmy hollered up at us.

"No, he's not up here," I said.

"Haven't seen him," Lenny said.

"Alright," Jimmy grumbled, then ran all through the camp, stopping everyone he saw to ask if they'd seen Mosquito.

"What do you think, Carl?" Lenny asked.

"I don't know, it looks pretty bad."

We learned later that Gibby, the platoon chief, had given Tyler permission to go out with the Marines without notifying Jimmy, so when the call came from EOD asking him to verify the whereabouts of Tyler Trahan (Mosquito), Jimmy was at a loss.

"Why the fuck didn't you tell me Mosquito was going out with the Marines?" Jimmy fumed at Gibby, when he finally located him playing video games in his hooch.

"Grandpa was supposed to tell you," he replied.

Little by little the mystery unfolded, and each new piece of information that came to light made me that much more enraged. It turned out the Marines had located a 155 artillery shell turned IED on the road and brought Mosquito up to have a look at it. He called it in and requested permission to blow it in place, because it looked too dangerous to move. The battle space commander denied his request and ordered him to take it back to base and blow it there, on the range. Mosquito protested, saying that there was no one around; it would be perfectly safe to detonate it where it was. The battle space commander wasn't having it. He ordered Mosquito to transport the 155 shell from the road back to base. When he went to move it, it went off.

I seethed for the better part of the day, screaming out loud, cursing the higher ups and their incompetence. Jimmy kept his distance from the rest of us for a while, knowing there was little he could say that would calm us down.

Mosquito was an EOD tech; his job was dangerous. But there was absolutely no upside to him bringing that fucking thing back to base and blowing it there. His death exemplified the failure of military bureaucracy. If the battle space commander had been out on that convoy, there's no way in hell he would have risked his own life transporting that IED. But because our new Standard Operating Procedure demanded we remove IEDs from "populated" areas (there were no civilians anywhere near that IED site) Tyler Trahan was needlessly sacrificed.

The grief and anger were too much, and the night and day difference between our operational tempo my first deployment and this standing-around-holding-our-dicks bullshit, coupled with the rage over Tyler's death, drove me to seek an outlet for my frustration. This would not be something just to pass the time, like the building of a trebuchet or a go-cart.

I began work on what would become my first book, *Battle on the Home Front*, around that time as a means of processing the feelings I'd experienced up to that point, but also to dime out those in the leadership whom I felt needed to be held to account. I knew voicing my outrage inside the camp wouldn't do any good because we all felt the same way and I didn't want to cause morale to sink any lower. This was my avenue.

THE BUTCHER OF FALLUJAH

The mood at Camp Schwedler had soured after Tyler's death. The routine of having to hand over intel to other units in the area because our leadership lacked the resolve to approve any real missions remained intact for most of the deployment. I recorded my observations in a journal, not realizing at the time that I would one day publish it.

We left the wire frequently, but no one fired a single shot. We had been told by our Commanding officer, Commander Gary Richards, who was later responsible for the most egregious courts martial in NSW history, "If you shoot someone, expect to answer to me."

One might argue that the lull in violence was the result of the successful "Surge" strategy implemented two years earlier, or the so called Sunni Awakening in which the local

Sunni tribes and militiamen ceased to aid Al Qaeda in Iraq and began working with American and Coalition forces instead of against them. But the fact was that America was pulling out of Iraq and we had become totally risk averse in the hopes of minimizing our collateral damage to avoid negative press for Obama.

At the same time, Afghanistan had begun heating up, and as far as the press was concerned, that was where the real war was. But there were still plenty of Al Qaeda in Iraq and other anti-coalition fighters in the area, and I knew that if we didn't deal with them now, one way or another, we would have to deal with them later.

In September, at the ass end of the deployment, our leadership was delivered the mission of the deployment. Our Assistant Officer-in-Charge (AOIC) Jason had put together a mission profile so compelling, even our war-wary head shed couldn't pass it up. One of our senior enlisted who'd been at HQ when the higher ups were discussing letting us hit this target told me, "I heard the words 'medal' and 'award' more than I heard anything about tactics." I was in shock when I first heard rumblings.

"You know, they're trying to get approval for us to go after that asshole Al-Isawi?" Lenny asked me, rhetorically.

"Who?"

"Al-Isawi, the Butcher of Fallujah. That motherfucker who killed those Blackwater guys, burned their bodies and hung them from the bridge over the Euphrates."

"Oh, yeah. I've heard of that shit bag. You think the head shed will pull their heads out of their asses to get it done?"

"Hope so."

Three of the four Blackwater guys were former SEALs. Everyone knew about Al-Isawi. He'd been on our radar for months. He was the guy that Chris Kyle was going after in the movie *American Sniper.*

And although our leadership was plagued with career obsessed officers who simply wanted to grind out the deployment without incident, we also had some good ones who wanted to get shit done, like Jason, our AOIC.

There were some stipulations for the op: we were going to have to take Iraqi Security Forces with us and make it look like they were in charge and we were just there for backup, which was bullshit, obviously. And though we had the legal authority to kill this guy if it came to that, the brass wanted him alive so he could stand trial in the Iraqi criminal courts. They were calling the op, Objective Amber. Aside from Osama Bin Laden, this guy was the most wanted terrorist in the world.

The second condition was that we had to have certain air assets: an AC130 Gunship, three helos, and an Intelligence-Surveilance-Reconnasaince (ISR) drone so our all-knowing commanders could micro manage our every move from the relative safety of their bunker. Jason and I spent twenty-four hours in the TOC allocating the air assets which were not easy to come by. As we were getting ready to roll out, we realized one of the helos had the wrong crypto loaded and would not be able to communicate with the other aircraft. I was senior JTAC now, so this was my responsibility. The op was almost scrubbed, but a Navy comms guy and I spent two hours gerry-rigging the radios till we got them to work properly. The whole time, the helos kept spinning their blades.

It was 0100 by the time we loaded onto the helos. The Iraqis, seventeen in total, were distributed between two aircraft. We didn't trust them, and we had reason not to. There had been way two many incidents of insider, or Green-on-Blue attacks in which Iraqi protégés had turned their weapons on their American or Coalition counterparts. We didn't suspect this would happen to us, but we weren't taking any chances, so we kept our eyes on them at all times, which actually made us more vulnerable because it meant we had to divert our focus—another real world example of politicians and lawyers running this war.

I was in the bird with Jimmy, Gonzales, Keefe, and Doc Paddy. Just as we got airborne, the helo lurched up and pitched violently to the right, and Keefe nearly went out the side door.

"Grab him!" Jimmy shouted.

"Got 'em," I said.

We learned later that the pilot had made a last minute maneuver to avoid a set of telephone lines that weren't on the map.

We touched down five klicks south of the target an hour and a half later. The helos made soft landings and our group of eight SEALs, fifteen Iraqi Army soldiers and two terps assembled into tactical formations. McCabe led a column of SEALs and Iraqis on the left flank and Lenny did the same on the right. Keefe and Burns were forward, doing recon, while Jimmy, Gonzales, and I formed the command and control element between the two columns.

The air temperature was hot for the predawn desert hours, which were usually much cooler. The sand was a fine powder, like moon dust, which muffled the sound of our footfalls. I was in constant contact with the air assets; the AC-130 covered our patrol while the ISR scouted ahead. I did this because we knew that the head shed in the TOC could only see the ISR feed, but did not maintain visual communication with the AC-130, and all the better, because if they had eyes on us, they would have wanted "feedback" from Jimmy every fifteen seconds.

I also did periodic radio checks with the TOC to maintain comms, but for the most part, everybody kept silent.

It felt good to be back out in the desert on the way to a target; on a real mission again. I was humping three radios, an amplifier, body armor, an M4 rifle, and Sig 226 pistol, three extra m4 mags, an extra pistol mag, a grenade, a flashbang, a slap charge for breaching, two water bottles (one in each cargo pocket), an izlid on my waist belt, a stripped down med kit, a pair of Nods, two Snickers bars, a flak jacket, a kevlar helmet and a Sat Comm antenna. You might call that a full combat load.

To their credit, the Iraqis were able to keep up without issue. We reached the city's outer perimeter about an hour later. It was a city in the middle of the desert. *What was it doing out here in the middle of nowhere? Was it a terrorist training camp?*

We gathered on a berm, 500 meters from the outer wall. Over the berm, the sand sloped down sharply into an exposed approach. There were giant flood lights mounted at the corners of the outer wall. The whole thing looked like a maximum security prison complex.

"How do you wanna do this?" Burns asked Jimmy.

"We'll just have to go for it, fire team by fire team."

"Roger that."

There was apprehension about how exposed we'd be on the approach to the city, but there was no other way of getting in. I had been monitoring the ISR, which had informed me of movement within the town.

"There's some movement inside, but it doesn't appear like any posturing," I said to Jimmy.

"Good to go."

We snuck down the sloping sand toward the wall, fire team by fire team, bounding overwatch toward the city's southern gate. Moving tactically around the outer perimeter, under the beam of the enormous floodlights, we eventually reached the entrance. ISR confirmed more movement of people outside on rooftops, but nothing tactical. Not yet. As we barreled through the city, people eyeballed us curiously and scurried away when they saw us coming, but no one adopted a defensive posture.

We located the building where Al-Isawi was alleged to be holed up, based on our intel. McCabe and Lenny smashed in the door with sledgehammers and entered the building with a few Iraqis and the terps.

I held cordon outside the door. The hairs on my neck began to stand up; I had a very bad feeling. The city lights were blurring out my Nods, so I folded them up because there was more than enough ambient light to see clearly.

I maintained communication with the ISR and the TOC while posted outside the target building. I was amazed no one had started shooting at us. The helos, waiting to extract us, had had to stop at a nearby base and refuel because of the fuel they'd wasted spinning their blades on the tarmac for two hours as we scrambled to get the comms to work. Murphy's Law 101.

With my back to the target building's front door, I could hear a physical altercation taking place inside. Someone (McCabe, probably) said, "Stay down!" and "Shut the fuck up!"

"Jackpot!" McCabe radioed to me a moment later, indicating Al-Isawi was in custody.

"Jackpot!" I relayed to the TOC.

I popped inside to see if they needed help clearing anything and there he was, Objective Amber, flexicuffed and sitting upright on the floor.

"Tell your boy nice job," Lenny said to me, referring to McCabe. "He tackled his ass. Shit bird had a gun, too!"

I laughed and headed back outside to keep the air assets and TOC in the loop. A few minutes later, Lenny and McCabe and the Iraqis and our terp came through the threshold of the building with Al-Isawi. His hands had been flexicuffed behind his back. I got a good look at his face before the blindfold and hood went on, it didn't have a scratch on it. And he didn't look like much.

"This motherfucker went for his .45. He's lucky I didn't shoot his ass!" McCabe said.

"What did you do?" I asked.

"I got the jump on him, so I tackled him and took it away." He smiled and produced the

.45 pistol.

"Good work, dude. Guess you're not such a bitch after all." I smirked and gave him a fist bump.

I couldn't believe he'd put himself at such great risk to bring this dirtbag in alive. I was incredibly proud.

"Warhawk 1-4, this is Zero-Five, requesting extract on secondary LZ."

"Roger that, Zero-Five. On our way."

The birds picked us up a short distance from the city's outer perimeter instead of the five klicks out where they'd dropped us off because there had been no shots fired and the risk of engagement was low.

"The Butcher of Fallujah, eh? He doesn't look like much."

TAKE IT ON THE CHIN

We made it back to base just as the sun was breaking over the horizon. Still wired from the op, we delivered Al-Isawi, AKA the Butcher of Fallujah, to a makeshift holding cell which consisted of a conex box with a locking gate. MA Westinson, the Navy cop assigned to the holding cell, took custody of Al-Isawi and Doc Paddy went in to give him a thorough physical examination. Doc Paddy was an Independent Duty Corpsman (IDC), so his medical expertise was advanced. The Navy considered him to be a healthcare provider, similar to a nurse practitioner or a physician's assistant.

He gave Al-Isawi a complete physical exam, head to toe, and determined that there was absolutely nothing medically wrong with him at the time of his transfer to the holding cell. Al-Isawi remained laconic from the moment we'd nabbed him. He knew the game; his jig was up.

Gonzales and McCabe and I went in and out of the holding cell a few times to be on hand if Doc Paddy or Westinson needed help with the prisoner for any reason. But the prisoner was extremely well behaved, so we walked a hundred feet to the chow hall and ate breakfast (or was it dinner?) and then went to our rooms to crash.

On this deployment, we each had our own quarters. I remember laying back, closing my eyes and drifting off for a while. But soon after I was awoken by the sound of someone banging on my door.

"What the fuck is it?"

I got up and opened the door.

"Jimmy wants everyone to muster at Danny's, now," Gonzales said with a concerned expression.

Danny's was a bar in San Diego—a popular West Coast SEAL hangout—after which the previous team had named the break room adjacent to the chow hall. It was where we hung out to kill time, but also where we had serious meetings, like this one was gearing up to be.

"What the fuck is going on, man? Did we get some follow-on intel or something?"

Unsure of the situation, I figured we were about to head back outside the wire for another op. It wouldn't have been the first time we'd had to go right back out.

"Nah, man. I don't know what's going on. Just put some shorts on and head to Danny's, I gotta go round up everyone else."

I was Gonales's best man at his wedding two years earlier. I knew he was a very even keeled dude. So, when I saw how wound up he was about the situation, it gave me cause for concern.

"Alright, man. I'll see you over there."

We were all at Danny's trying to figure out what the fuck was going on when Jimmy stormed in, steaming mad, and shouted, "Anyone wanna fucking explain this?"

He held up a blood-stained rag.

"What is that?" I asked.

"It's that fucking guy's dash, man. The man-dress that he was wearing when we got him. It's all bloody. He's saying you guys beat him up, please tell me it's not true!"

Jimmy's voice was trembling. A mixture of fear and rage shaped his words. I spoke up first.

"Whoa, I don't know what's going on here, but nobody would do this to you. None of us would put you in this position."

"Yeah, we didn't do that shit," Lenny said. Everyone nodded in agreement.

"Yo, if one of us hit him, there'd be a lot more blood than that," Keefe said, which made sense coming from a 6'3", 250-pound SEAL.

"Yeah," McCabe said. "No shit."

Jimmy looked us each in the eye.

"I believe you. I'm gonna take care of this. But I have to report this shit. Wait here." Jimmy dropped the bloody rag on the floor and walked out.

"Man, can you believe this bullshit?" McCabe said.

"None of you hit him, right?"

"Fuck no, Carl!" Gonzales said.

"Neither did I, but I had to ask once."

"How did he get that thing all bloody?" Keefe asked, pointing to the dishdasha on the floor. "What, do you think he, like, smashed his face into the wall or bit his lip or some shit like that?"

We all stood there, thinking about it.

"I mean, how else could he have gotten blood on it? Where was Westinson, wasn't he supposed to be watching him?" I asked.

In that moment, I made the decision to one day publish *Battle on the Home Front*, which had, up to that point, been little more than a personal log of events. I wanted to be able to tell my side of the story, because I knew at this point, things were about to go bad. We waited at Danny's for a half hour or so before Jimmy came bursting back inside.

"You guys gotta transfer this guy to the Iraqi Police station. But first, I need everyone of you to fill out shooter statements in the TOC."

Shooter statements were standard protocol for after a high profile op, so nobody thought too much about them. After all, it was our opportunity to explain things the way we remembered them. It was all internal at that point, and the statements were inadmissible in court unless we'd been read our rights (which we had not) so we had very little reason to fear. We each handwrote our personal accounts of the op, turned them in to Jimmy, then took that dirt bag Al-Isawi to the IP station.

The station house was located north of Fallujah, a city, which, at one point, was the scene of the some of the most intense fighting in the entire war. But that was years earlier in '04. In post-Surge, pre-ISIS Iraq, Fallujah was still hot, but not as bad as it had been.

"We just fucking caught this guy," Gonzales spoke up, "the guy we've been looking for for years and we're just gonna turn him over and that's that?"

What Gonzales was worried about, what we all were worried about, was that once we dropped Al-Isawi off at the IP station, that would be the last anybody ever saw of him.

"Yeah, that's right," Jimmy said dispassionately.

But we were men who did things when we were told to, and Jimmy had told us to bring Al-Isawi to the IP station, so that's what we did. Only, we didn't leave him there. How could we? It took us over five years just to get intel on this guy's location. There was no way we were taking any chances leaving him with the IPs.

When we got to the station house, Al-Isawi started acting differently. All of a sudden his head hurt and he had trouble walking. He started wailing like a hurt puppy, and we all looked at each other, like *what the fuck?*

The IPs were visibly afraid of him. When they realized who he was, they didn't want anything to do with him. They knew he was dangerous and feared he still had the power to hurt them and their loved ones, even in captivity. So we hung around the station for ten fucking hours, babysitting him.

After some internal discord, we finally left the station house and drove back to Camp Schwedler. "Well, the IPs have him" was the general consensus of our command. I hit the chow hall as soon as we got back and lumbered to my room in a state between sleep and consciousness. I'd been running on fumes the last few hours, and it had taken its toll.

I slept soundly through the night and awoke the next morning to learn the IPs were too scared to hold onto Al-Isawi, and that they wanted us to come get him. *What the fuck? Are they serious?* I thought.

So, we picked him up and brought him to a high-level detention center in Baghdad. On the ride over, he was in my truck. He didn't say a word. He was thin as a beanpole, over six feet tall, in his early forties. There was an ominous quality to his presence. For all his terror and bloodshed, he was no longer a danger to US and coalition forces or citizens of Iraq. But his erroneous accusations against us made him a threat to our integrity, and that was something we took very seriously.

We turned him over to the detention center in Baghdad, which was an actual jail with cells as opposed to a conex box with bars on it like we had back at Camp Schwedler, and that was that. As far as I was concerned, we were done with him.

When we got back to base, Westinson started acting really weird and saying some stupid shit that got us all worried.

"They're gonna fuck us, man! We're all gonna go to jail!"

"Relax, man," Keefe said. "None of us laid a finger on that guy, no one's going to jail. You need to chill the fuck out and stop talking that bullshit, for real."

The day-to-day in the camp had been interrupted. There was a cloud of uncertainty that hung heavy over everyone involved in Objective Amber that seemed to grow larger and more troublesome the more time wore on. Further opping was out of the question. In the operational sense, our deployment had effectively ended the night we captured that high-value target, Isawi, the Butcher of Fallujah. What we were experiencing now was some sort of administrative purgatory. Very serious allegations had been levied against us, but no one had corroborated Al-Isawi's story; it was our word against his, and we would naturally prevail, I believed, because the truth was on our side.

"I've got some bad news," Jimmy addressed us all at Danny's. "Westinson said you beat this guy up."

"What the fuck?!" We all shouted in unison.

"Stay away from him, don't go near him. I know you all probably want to kill him, but give him space. Let me sort this out." He looked right at me and said, "You got that, Carl?"

"Yes, sir."

The fact that I said "sir" to Jimmy really underscored the severity of the situation. After all, we called him "Jimmy," not "Lieutenant" or "sir." I was seething mad, ready to rip Westinson's heart out. *How could he fucking lie like that?!*

I've had years to mull over the accusations Master at Arms 3rd Class Westinson made against my fellow SEALs and I, and the tidal wave of controversy which followed. My belief is that he cooked up this story to cover his own ass, because it came out that he had left his post more than once while Al-Isawi was in his custody, and if he blamed it on someone else, his dereliction of duty would be overlooked.

So, because of this asshole and his lying mouth, all eight SEALs from the Objective Amber op had to go to Team 10 headquarters in Ramadi to go over our shooter statements with John Stamp, a Navy Criminal Investigative Service (NCIS) civilian agent. Stamp was an average guy; white, bald, early thirties. His office was a standard wooden hut with an unfinished wood desk somebody probably cut for him at the wood shop on post, like virtually all of the offices in-country.

He met with us one at a time, while the rest hung back at the front of the hut and bullshitted.

"I can't fucking believe we're talking to NCIS. Is this a joke?" Keefe said.

"It'll be over soon," I said, optimistically.

When it was my turn to go back there, I followed Stamp to his desk and sat down across from him.

"Hi, Carl."

"Hi."

"As I'm sure you're well aware by now, this is a very serious matter. We'd like you to rewrite your shooter statement so we can get a better idea of exactly what went on during the op and afterward."

"What's wrong with the first one?"

"Oh, there's nothing wrong with the first one, it's just that we think it would help move the situation along if you rewrote your statement."

What the fuck is this guy talking about? I figured that he was trying to pull some kind of Jedi mind trick to get me to confess to something I didn't do and implicate my teammates in the process.

"You've got my statement."

"I know, but..."

"You've got my statement."

"Very well, then let's go over it again."

We went back and forth for a little while. He tried to pull his *NCIS, Law & Order* bullshit on me, but I wasn't having it. As stressful a situation as that was, I was able to rest easy and just be honest, because I knew that me and my guys were in the right and had nothing to lie about. The truth was on our side, this whole thing would get cleared up sooner or later. Besides, from my impression of Stamp, it seemed that despite his job, he knew the deal.

We learned later from Doc Paddy, who'd been cleared of any wrongdoing and returned to Camp Schwedler, that Keefe, McCabe, Gonzales, and Doc Paddy were brought into the TOC at Ramadi, a huge space teeming with high tech surveillance equipment and computer screens with grainy drone feeds, and stripped of their weapons and gear by Master Chief Wilskey—the Team 7 Command Master Chief (CMC)—and placed on administrative hold pending a full investigation of the alleged incident.

When I learned of this betrayal later on at Camp Schwedler I was overcome with rage. It felt totally surreal. I literally couldn't believe what was happening. We had worked so hard, pushed ourselves to the max and beyond, both in training and in the field, had put ourselves at risk too many times to count, and these fuckers were throwing us under the bus on the say-so of some dirtbag terrorist and a lowlife Master at Arms who'd admitted to abandoning his post. My only recourse was to keep a documented record, the screed that would later become *Battle on the Homefront*.

The days at Camp Schwedler were filled with tension and listlessness. I talked to Kaitlyn a little bit about what was going on, but I didn't go into great detail because I didn't want her to worry.

A few days after our initial interview with NCIS, we were brought back to Ramadi and read our rights. We weren't handcuffed, but we were technically under arrest. Westinson had been removed from Camp Schwedler for his own protection, and rightfully so.

When we got to Ramadi, I returned to the NCIS hut and sat across the unfinished wood desk from Agent Stamp as he, once more, tried to get me to falsely incriminate myself.

"Let's talk about your statement."

"Lawyer."

"You sure you want to get a lawyer involved in this? It just makes you look guiltier. Once you open this can of worms, there's no going back. I'll give you one more chance to talk."

"Lawyer!" I hollered, slamming my fist down on the desk.

"Have it your way. Don't say I didn't warn you."

"Fuck you! Whose team are you on, asshole?" I hollered.

I conferred later with everyone else from the op who'd been interrogated by Stamp. He tried every trick in the book to get us to rat out other members of the platoon. He threatened us with jail time, dishonorable discharge from the Navy, and anything else he could think of. What he failed to realize is that we would literally die to save one of our own. In fact, that's the standard of service, not just for SEALs, but for all fighting servicemen. And, we were innocent, so we had no reason to lie. To this day I genuinely believe that Stamp made the recommendation to not pursue this case, but rather word trickled down to us from another member of the command that Commander Gary Richards said something to the effect of, "I don't care what your report says, find something on these guys, my career will not be marked by this."

For the duration of our deployment, we made upwards of ten trips to Ramadi to deal with these bogus allegations. On one such trip I ran into Gonzales, Keefe, and McCabe. They looked awful.

"Hey, how are you guys doing?"

"Carl, you wouldn't believe the bullshit they're making us do," Gonzales said.

"Dude, this is fucking *Groundhog Day*. We wake up, sweep the dirt. It never ends."

"That sucks, man."

"Whatever," Keefe said. "They can't keep us here forever."

I was amazed at how they'd managed to keep their spirits up. They'd effectively been put on a working party, cleaning up the base and moving stuff around. These were highly trained Special Operators, experienced fighters who'd taken part in one of the most high profile ops in the post-9/11 era, and they'd been reduced to the status of glorified janitors.

"Listen, if there's anything you need..."

"Don't sweat it man," Gonzales said. "We'll beat this bullshit."

To this day, I think he was legitimately worried I was going to stage an armed rebellion against the chain of command, and I would have. Master Chief Wilskey, the same man who'd personally ordered Gonzales, Keefe, and McCabe to surrender their weapons and body armor, was doing turnover with the SEAL Team 3 CMC and decided to take the opportunity to address the remaining SEALs from Objective Amber. He had us muster at Danny's, then dropped it on us.

"Look, you guys gotta own this. You made some mistakes, that's fine. Be a man, own up to it. Take it on the chin." He paused a minute. "But if you go the route of the lawyers, it's gonna be a bad day for you," he said, then broke off to talk to Jimmy.

What he was trying to do was get us to accept a Non-Judicial Punishment (NJP), also called Captain's Mast in the Navy. In an NJP scenario, the accused stand before the commanding officer and are able to make their case, but they can't call witnesses or cross examine the prosecution's witness. In fact, there is no prosecutorial body. In effect, the commanding officer is judge and jury.

The benefit of electing to stand for NJP is that the worst thing they can do is bust you down two ranks, restrict your duty and dock your pay for sixty days. The alternative to NJP is to request a court martial, which is a military trial-by-jury with an impartial judge who is in no way affiliated with the command. In a court martial, the accused may hire a lawyer, call witnesses, and exercise due process within the limitations of the Uniform Code of Military Justice (UCMJ) and you are actually innocent until proven guilty. The downside to a court martial is that they can really throw the book at you. Worst case scenario, they can sentence you to death. This rarely happens; the last person to receive a death sentence under the UCMJ was the coward, Major Nidal

Hassan, who opened fire on a group of unarmed soldiers at a pre-deployment processing center inside Fort Hood, TX.

We weren't facing a death penalty, but Master Chief Wilskey strongly implied we'd be looking at hard time in Leavenworth, and would likely incur a Bad Conduct or Dishonorable Discharge from the Navy, which would make us ineligible to vote in any election, or own property or firearms for the rest of our lives. Also, we would lose all of our veterans benefits like the GI Bill or follow-on health care for the many injuries we'd sustained throughout our military careers.

When he walked off, we huddled together and tried to make sense of things.

"Fuck this shit, I'm not going to Captain's Mast," I said.

"They want to NJP my ass, fuck 'em! I'll request courts martial, we'll see how they like that!" Lenny said.

"Uh-huh," everyone agreed.

On a subsequent trip to Camp Schwedler, Master Chief Wilskey told us, "When we find out you're lying, you're all getting charged with obstruction of justice."

This was a total conflict of interest. As Command Master Chief for SEAL Team 7, Wilskey was legally obligated to remain impartial to the question of our guilt or innocence, because he represented the legal body that would preside over our trial, should we elect to go the route of NJP, which none of us did for obvious reasons.

It'd been weeks since anyone had heard from Gonzales, McCabe, or Keefe. Master Chief had intimated that there was a possibility they'd be turned over to the Iraqi criminal justice system. When word of this spread, we came to a consensus that if that was the case, we were going to convoy out to Ramadi and break them out of jail ourselves regardless of who was in our way. Mutiny or not, we weren't about to let the leadership turn our brothers over to the Iraqis, no way! This was likely a ruse on their part to get us to cop to something because they had no real evidence against us. At this point I had spoken to the other SEALs on the FOB about the reality of an armed rescue mission from our own leadership, the way it might play out and what the ramifications would be.

With the uncertainty of our futures looming over us like ominous storm clouds, the Baharia detachment of Echo Platoon, SEAL Team 10 broke down our camp, loaded up our gear into RG-33s and up-armored flatbeds and convoyed out to Al Assad, three hours to the west through endlessly flat desert. Keefe, Gonzales, and McCabe were still being detained by the time we flew out. Rumor had it they'd been flown to Qatar and were subjected to more humiliating manual labor. The reality of it was that our head shed wanted them as isolated from us as possible in the hopes that it would crush their spirits.

We had a three-day layover in Rota, Spain. Mandatory fun, we called it. The idea was that we'd unwind a bit before going home and seeing our families. I think they were afraid we'd kill our spouses or some nonsense like that, so they stuck us by the pool in Rota and gave us unlimited access to booze, which we took full advantage of. As I said before, I'm not a big drinker, but some other guys got so fucked up they fell out of their chairs and rolled into the pool and almost had to be rescued. It was slightly demoralizing to watch guys with so much experience in water survival nearly drown in a swimming pool because they'd drunk themselves into a bottomless stupor.

When we got back to Little Creek, there was a lightning storm, so the civilian air crew wouldn't unload our stuff. We sat inside the airport, our loved ones waiting on the other side of an opaque glass wall, unable to clear customs because our gear was still on the plane. After three hours we went up to the head customs guy and told him if he didn't let us through we were going through anyway. He let us through.

Kaitlyn was waiting for me.

"Let's go home, Kait."

"Okay."

THE TRIALS

I'd be lying if I said it didn't feel a little awkward with Kaitlyn at first. In the year and a half we'd been married, I'd spent no more than two months by her side, and I felt uncomfortable that we weren't as close as I'd wished we'd been. Going forward, we were going to live for the first time like a normal couple, and that frightened me, because it was a new experience and I wanted more than anything for it to work.

I went on post-deployment leave and got called into headquarters almost every day again because they knew I didn't leave the area and would be on hand to supervise this or help with that, or whatever. After I came back from leave, I checked out of Team 10 and into Detachment Little Creek, a training command that would allow me to chill for at least two years without deploying. In the Navy, this is called a shore duty billet. A deployable unit, like SEAL Team 10, is considered a sea duty billet. It's possible for guys to get deployed from shore duty, but it's rare. The plan was to take this time to start a family, and improve my physical fitness to screen for Dam Neck—otherwise known as SEAL Team 6—the most elite unit in the world.

I hadn't been charged with prisoner abuse, but the whole incident had left me in a sort of legal limbo. As a result, some of the Team 10 guys looked at me funny as I was checking out. Likewise, when I checked into Det Little Creek, I could tell the head shed had all heard about what happened. I felt stigmatized, like they thought I was some sort of dirt bag, and it really pissed me off. *How much longer do I have to keep putting up with this bullshit? So much for innocent until proven guilty!* I thought.

The last time I'd checked into a new command, I did so in my dress blues as was protocol, and the Petty Officer of the Watch (POW) screamed "Cyclops!" and made me jump into the surf and get sandy on the way out. This time, I showed up in cammies.

"Hey, I'm Carl. Checking in."

"Hey, Carl, welcome to Det Little Creek."

I was a second class petty officer now, a two-platooner with significant combat experience, a squad leader and a senior JTAC. By this point, I'd paid my dues. There would be no *Cyclops* this time around.

One thing that impressed me about Det Little Creek is that they put photos of all the SEALs and guys under SEAL commands who'd been killed in the post-9/11 War on Terror on the back wall of the quarter deck, behind the POWs desk. Immediately, I recognized Tyler, J. Louie, Bobby, and Steven. *I'm not here to replace them,* I thought, *because they're irreplaceable.*

Krom was my LPO again at Det Little Creek. In fact, he was the one who helped me get orders in the first place. It was good to see someone from the early days.

"What is this bullshit I keep hearing about with that asshole from Fallujah?"

"It's just a bunch of nonsense. Some dipshit MA lied and said McCabe hit the guy while he was in custody, so everyone's got their panties in a bunch."

"Did he do it?"

"Fuck no!"

"Alright."

Everyone from the Teams who wasn't there for the sake of their own career reacted the same way when they heard about the situation. They'd ask if the allegations were true, because, they figured, why would this ass clown Westinson cook the whole thing up? And when I'd tell them that no way, no how did anyone from the op lay a finger on Al-Isawi other than to capture and transport him back to Camp Schwedler, they'd believe me, unlike our leadership.

At my new job, I would teach two classes: Helicopter Rope Suspension Techniques (HRST) and Static Line Jumpmaster. In order to teach them, I had to first audit them. But before I could do that, I had to attend a Navy leadership course called Journeyman. It was located at Dam Neck Base, just outside the headquarters for SEAL Team 6, the place I'd hoped to catch orders to after Det Little Creek. Oddly enough, I was the only SEAL taking the course.

The rest of the guys were cooks, mechanics, or Masters at Arms—essentially the rank and file. The last time I had anything to do with the regular Navy was bootcamp, six years earlier. The Navy is staffed with good technicians-competent professionals who do their jobs well. But they don't do what SEALs do, and their standard of excellence is not what ours is.

When I showed up to the course (in my dress blues) the chief there tried to tell me that my Body Mass Index was out of regulations, which made me laugh. The Navy and their draconian system of measuring body fat meant taking four measurements; height, weight, neck and waist circumference and plugging them into a basic mathematical equation. By this method, at 240 pounds and six feet tall, I was considered nearly forty percent body fat. Knowing full well that I hover around eight percent body fat, I protested them dropping me from the class on the basis of their arbitrary analysis. So, they had me do a Physical Readiness Test (PRT) right there on the spot, in my dress blues!

The truth is that while all Navy jobs require skill and due diligence, very few of them are physically demanding. But my job was, so I took care to always be in shape. And the Navy PRT which consisted of two minutes of push-ups, two minutes of sit-ups and a one and a half mile run wasn't exactly a strenuous challenge.

The Journeyman course itself was just a basic leadership course. Everything they taught — lead by example, hold your people accountable, etc. — I'd learned through experience with the Teams.

Journeyman course completed, I audited the HRST and Static Line Jumpmaster courses back to back, then got to work as an instructor, which was a great experience. HRST, especially, was a good course because it taught real life, applicable skills, like fast roping. Fast roping is when an operator inserts on a target by sliding down a rope. We wear mechanic's gloves so the friction doesn't peel our skin off and we learn a technique for guiding the rope between our feet, but that's pretty much it. I had fast roped into combat situations on my first deployment, so I knew that it was an effective tactic.

Rappelling, on the other hand, requires a harness, and is a much more cumbersome method of insertion by comparison. In fact, the only practical application for rappelling would be if an operator had to really have total control of his descent down a long rope, or during a rescue scenario. I had to teach both methods, even though rappelling was something that not a single operator I knew had ever done in a real life situation.

The Static Line Jumpmaster course was a prerequisite for Free Fall Jumpmaster; a sort of preliminary certification. This is the one that you see in the movies where there are guys on a plane (one of them is usually throwing up) and there's a line that runs from the back of the plane out through the open door. The guys on the plane are connected to the (static) line by the rip cord of their parachutes, and when they jump out of the plane, the weight of their bodies pulls the cord and opens the chute. This method of insertion is problematic and rarely used in real life situations as an insertion technique. But anyone who wants to be Free Fall Jumpmaster qualified has to first complete the Static Line course.

The SEALs who went through my course understood that they were checking a box, going through the motions. Some of them were higher ranked with more experience than me. I recognized the tediousness of this course and did my best to mitigate the bullshit. But, I demanded a high standard of excellence from them, and they delivered. A few of the men who came through my Static Line course were SEAL Team 6 guys who were later killed when that bird went down in Afghanistan in 2011, three months after the Osama Bin Laden op. Their photos went up on the wall of the Quarterdeck and I saw them everyday after that, when I would pause to pay my respects when coming through the door.

Over the next few months, as the drama of the situation with Al-Isawi festered, I made frequent trips to Naval Special Warfare (NSW) Group 2 headquarters to speak with the legal hacks there. They kept trying to get me to cave.

"You know, Carl, if you did see something, this whole thing could get cleared up quickly."

"You have my statement."

In October, Keefe, Gonzales, and McCabe finally got back from Qatar. I went over to Gonzales's house to say hello and find out what I could about the whole ordeal.

"This is fucking bullshit," he said.

"What's going on?"

"I'm not supposed to talk to anyone about it, but I'll tell you, man, this is garbage, what they're putting me through."

I also learned from Gonzales that Westinson had made additional statements since we'd last seen him. He was now implicating me and two others, but the understanding was that the prosecution would not proceed with charges to additional people at this point.

I saw Keefe around the same time and McCabe about a week later. McCabe was who they were really after, because according to Westinson's false statement, he was the one that slugged Al-Isawi. Only now, the story was that he punched him in the stomach, which failed to explain the (self-inflicted) cut on Al-Isawi's lip.

Prior to deployment, McCabe had started dating a blonde bombshell named Holly. She managed to get her hooks in him pretty quickly; a few months after deployment they were engaged. The idea that he was involved in a major news media story really excited her. I could tell she was trouble, but there was no getting through to McCabe. Even a highly-trained and experienced elite warrior is no match for a beautiful woman.

By January, the story had broken in the media, and luckily, they were on our side. We were notified that a February courts martial for Keefe and Gonzales was imminent. And we were all going to be flown out to Baghdad so Al-Isawi, the terrorist who murdered three former SEALs and a former Army Ranger and strung them up on the bridge in Fallujah, could have his day in court. McCabe's trial, the more serious of the three, would be held in Little Creek, after the trials in Baghdad had concluded.

The trials got pushed back to April 2010 because the prosecution didn't want to declassify the shooter statements we'd given after the event. The issue here was that our defense attorneys could not review the evidence against their clients, making a trial impossible. The military continually maintained that they didn't have to turn those over; this may have stemmed from their overall incompetence or their limited understanding of actual law. Eventually, the defense won out, and our statements became a matter of public record.

A week or so after the documents were declassified and sent to our attorneys, all of us were notified that our personal information, including full names, addresses, Social Security numbers, etc. had "inadvertently been made public," and were now all over the Internet. Coincidence? We didn't think so.

I had started a tree service business and began moonlighting at a local gym on weekends to make a little extra cash on the side. I found that I was my best self when I kept busy, so that's what I did.

In January, I met Guy for the first time. He was a Judge Advocate General (JAG)—a military lawyer—who was representing Gonzales in the courts martial. I had not been charged myself, but my future was anything but certain. The status was that I *could* be charged with prisoner abuse, obstruction of justice, or making false statements, and I carried that stress around for months leading up to the trial.

"Now Carl, I think at this point the Navy is just trying to cover its own ass. That said, they can still try to bring the hammer down on you, but they don't have much of a case."

"I didn't do anything wrong. None of us did anything wrong."

"I believe you, but it's not what you know, it's what you can prove. And the Navy is going to have a hard time proving that anyone of you struck that prisoner, so I think we're in good shape. I just want to prepare you for the worst, so there aren't any surprises."

"I understand."

For the first time, it seemed, someone from the regular Navy believed we were telling the truth and was willing to stand up for us. Guy was a true rockstar; he spoke of honor like it actually meant something, and lived by a high moral code. If anyone could get us out of this mess, it was him.

A month later the SEALs from the Objective Amber op were back together again, this time at the Norfolk airport awaiting a flight to Qatar by way of DC, and eventually on to Baghdad.

"Follow me to the bar!" Doc Paddy shouted, so we all followed.

"Alright guys," Jimmy said after a few rounds. "Let's try to keep it together..."

"Shots!" someone shouted.

"Yeah, more shots!" Keefe echoed.

"Fuck it," Jimmy said, giving into the shenanigans.

We stayed there in the airport bar getting good and tight for a few hours before our flight arrived.

"Holy shit, is that Westinson?" I said, pointing to a figure moving through the airport, conspicuously avoiding eye contact with all of us.

"Yeah, that's him," Jason said. "Who's that ass clown next to him?"

"Must be his handler," I said. "Or his boyfriend, hahahaha!" We all laughed.

Despite our mild drunkenness, which may or may not have caused a minor scene at the airport, we gave Westinson a wide berth the whole way to Baghdad. The last thing any of us wanted was to hand him a moral victory by beating his ass. And seeing as he was (falsely) accusing us of being rough with a prisoner, it would have compromised our credibility as witnesses if someone broke his jaw, regardless of whether or not he deserved it.

When we arrived in DC, we kept drinking for a few more hours before boarding our next flight. The plane ride to Qatar was long, as trips to the Middle East often are.

The plane was packed with people of Middle Eastern descent; we were the only Americans onboard. We got the sense that they didn't much want us around, but we had a few drinks and kept our spirits up anyway. I took two Ambien, a Flexoril and drank another beer, and woke up in Doha. Also,

I gave Guy the complete first draft of *Battle on the Home Front* and he read it on the plane ride over, even with all the legal work he had to do for the trial.

"Carl, if you publish this, they're going to hammer you, you know that?"

"So be it. I have to get this out."

Qatar is considered downrange, so they had to issue us flak jackets and Kevlar helmets once we arrived at the main US base there. It felt strange to be wearing a vest, but not carrying a rifle or pistol. I felt vulnerable, not that there was any great threat stalking us in Doha.

We spent three days in the transient tents, bullshitting and catching up. I went to breakfast at the chow hall one morning and sat down next to an older guy, either a high ranking officer or senior enlisted.

"How's it going?" I said, cordially.

"Good morning," he answered.

Definitely an officer. A colonel, maybe.

"You here for this fucking courts martial, too? What a crock of shit!"

He smirked, but didn't say anything. I proceeded to tell him my involvement in the case, how there was no way, no how any of us would have done it, least of all Gonzales. Finally, he cracked.

"Seems dumb," he said in a low tone. "It's unrealistic."

I could sense from his age and his reserved stance on the subject that he was somehow involved in the case, probably at the leadership level. So, I took the opportunity to let him hear my piece, making sure I didn't say anything too over the top, though remaining true to my feelings of anger and frustration at the whole ordeal.

Outside the trailers where we were being housed, I bumped into one of the prosecution's JAGs, a woman in her early thirties. She was staring me down, perhaps wondering if I had the balls to say something.

"Is there something I can do for you, ma'am?"

I'd gone most of my career without smarting off at those appointed over me. I was no longer a new guy, and I was good enough at my job that I rarely put my superiors in a position to give me lectures. But the stress of this whole ridiculous, surreal situation really began to bear down on me, and finally, I snapped.

"You're not even supposed to be talking to me!" she shouted.

"Yeah?" I shouted back. "Well you're not supposed to be throwing a fellow service member under the bus like this!"

"You have your job, I have mine! My job is to prosecute your friends for what happened in that cell at camp Schwedler!"

"You know what my job is, ma'am? God forbid, you get kidnapped like Jessica Lynch, my job is to find out where you are and come get your ass. That's *my* job!"

"You're not supposed to be talking to me, you better stop right now and walk away or I'm going to take this up the chain of command!"

"You just flew me half way around the fucking world for this courts martial, what are you going to do now, take away my birthday?" I laughed as Guy came running up to step in.

"Carl, what the fuck are you doing? You're still in the Navy!" he said, escorting me away.

"Fuck her," I said, loudly enough for her to hear as I walked off.

The next day we took a C-130 flight to Baghdad. C-130s aren't built for comfort, anyone who's ever flown in one knows that. Unlike the much larger C-17, occupants of a C-130 must sit in rows that run lengthwise on the edges of the cabin, facing each other. There's hardly any room at all, each passenger has his knee in the crotch of the guy across from him. And on this flight, it was that son-of-a-bitch Westinson sitting across from me, his head down the whole way from Doha to Baghdad, not daring to lock eyes with me.

He was flanked on either side by lawyers, as was I. The thought occurred to me, that if I'd had a little less self control, I might have reached across the aisle and choked the life out of him before anyone would have been able to stop me. But I did have self control, and so did Gonzales, Keefe, and McCabe. We were warriors, not henchmen. So I sat there mean mugging him the entire flight.

We arrived in Baghdad in the middle of the night, and walked half a mile in the dark to our berthing units, which were two-man trailers. My roommate was a Navy master-at-arms, like Westinson. In fact, he was Westinson's boss. He spoke openly about what a dirtbag Westinson was, and how he wasn't at all surprised that he'd cooked up this cockamamie story. It was a relief to know that not everyone believed the hype.

We held the first official muster for all those involved in the courts martial outside the barracks the day after we'd arrived. The older officer I was bullshitting with at the chowhall in Qatar turned out to be the judge! *Well whatever.*

It was still a few days before the trials began, so Keefe and I went to the gym a lot and both broke the base record for bench, squat, and deadlift — one rep of each. I did over 1,700 pounds total, he did around 1,500; chalk that up to the anger over the case, I guess.

The first trial, Gonzales's, began the following day. All the witnesses for the defense were put in a room off to the side of the courthouse, which was a simple wood structure like most other offices on base. We were there for two days, sitting around looking at each other. They'd told us not to talk, so we whispered. Guy was reluctant to put me on the stand because he thought I might fly off the handle and start lecturing the court on values like honor and constitutional freedom, so I wound up not getting called in the first trial.

Around noon on the second day, the trial was over, Gonzales had won!

As the verdict was read, there were a ton of higher ups in the courtroom that were extremely disappointed with the way things had played out. CDR Richards even stormed out. I'm sure he was thinking, *how will this affect my career?* We were all very happy. Other SEALs that were stationed in Baghdad at the time came to the trials in a show of solidarity. It was an awesome victory, but we still had one more to go.

I'd seen Al-Isawi being ferreted around to give testimony, through a translator, against Keefe and Gonzales. They'd blindfolded him, but he kept a shit-eating grin on his face the whole time. They couldn't keep him in the room with us, for obvious reasons, so they kept him in a separate room with Westinson, his new best friend!

The next day, the judge dismissed the jury and invoked sua sponte, a legal term meaning "of its own accord." He had sat through the first trial in which Guy eviscerated Westinson on the stand, by systematically punching holes in his story, destroying what little credibility he had left. He believed he had a good enough understanding of the case to conduct the trial himself. And that's what he did. I spent most of the time in the quiet room, but after a few hours, I was called to the stand. It was just the judge and I going back and forth. Neither the defense nor the prosecution examined me.

"Petty Officer Higbie, did you see Petty Officer McCabe strike the prisoner, Ahmed Hashim Abd Al-Isawi?"

"No, sir."

"Do you see this trial as a travesty of justice?"

"Yes, sir. This is a complete black eye, not only for my peers, but to the US military in general. And it's a slap in the face to our citizens. The chain of command has abused its power to..."

"OK," he cut me off.

"How would you describe Petty Officer Gonzales's character?"

"I was the Best Man at Petty Officer Gonzales's wedding. He is a close friend and an excellent teammate. I can say without a shred of doubt that he is the most honest person I've ever met. And I think the charges against him are ludicrous."

It went on like this for about ten minutes. As I recall, many of the questions were simple yes or no and I answered them in a cool, reserved manner. Guy was pleased that I didn't cause a scene or break something.

I returned to the witness room after my testimony, satisfied that I'd gone on record denying the bogus allegations made against my teammates. Less then an hour later, it was over. Gonzales had won! It was a huge victory for us, now we could celebrate. McCabe still had his trial coming up, but with the complete exoneration of Keefe and Gonzales, the prosecution truly had no case.

I wondered what was going on in Westinson's head when first the jury, then the judge, completely invalidated his testimony, basically asserting that he was a liar. How could he go back to work and face everybody after something like that? Who would ever trust him again?

Both trials complete, the SEALs from Objective Amber (minus McCabe, who'd stayed home to prepare for his own trial) and the SEALs stationed in Baghdad celebrated in earnest. There was no drinking because we were in Baghdad and that wasn't allowed, but there was a lot of hooting and hollering. A lot of "Fuck you for doubting us!" rants shouted up into the air as an expression of release that after all this time, we'd finally made it through.

It took us a few days to break down everything and head out to Qatar, where we chilled out for another few days allowing the victory to soak in. Had things gone the other way, we would be headed home minus two men, Gonzales and Keefe. Despite the fact that it was absurd these trials took place to begin with, my faith in the system was somewhat restored by the outcome. I had found a good friend in Guy. I didn't realize it at the time, but our paths would cross once more in the not-too-distant future.

We boarded the passenger plane that would return to DC, our nation's capital; the nation we loved and served.

THE RUNAROUND

Everyone was in high spirits following the vindication of Gonzales and Keefe. McCabe's subsequent court-martial, which took place locally in Little Creek, was a joke. The defense's star witness, Westinson, had been so thoroughly discredited by Guy and the other defense lawyers in Baghdad, the prosecution didn't have a leg to stand on. Their case had been weak to begin with, but Westinson's prior testimony made it hopeless, which was great news for us.

Everybody was happy this whole mess was over and now we could get back to our lives. I was a lucky man; my life thus far had been fortuitous. I'd survived two combat deployments with SEAL Team 10 and our command's attempt to destroy us and I was ready to start a family. Everything was working out.

But still, I felt an obligation to publish my journal. For Tyler, for all the bullshit we had to deal with following the Objective Amber op, for every Rule of Engagement that had been codified and adopted by bureaucrats and politicians in DC who'd never even held a rifle or knew what it felt like to be shot at, I had to make our voices heard. And as I'd learn, it would be an arduous process fraught with tension and obstruction by those same bureaucrats.

Because I was a Special Operator, I had a security clearance and was privy to information that should by all means remain guarded, and I knew that. But I also knew that I had rights as a citizen, that chief among them was my First Amendment right to free speech. I never in my wildest dreams would even contemplate divulging any classified material or information relating to Operational Security (OPSEC), but I was determined to publish my polemic of government and military practices and procedures, *Battle on the Home Front*.

The challenge I had before me was getting my chain of command to review my book, determine that there were no OPSEC violations, and sign off on it so I could have it published. However, my book openly criticized the American government and military, and no one in my chain of command wanted to be the one who signed off on the book that made people look bad. So they gave me the runaround.

The first thing I did when I got back from the courts martial in Baghdad was notify my master chief, Master Chief Black, that I intended to publish a book about what I'd experienced. This was April 2010. He was initially dismissive of my ambition, but in the end, said that he would get back to me with a point-of-contact for where and how to start the vetting process. He never did.

For the next few months, he and I went back and forth. Although Black seemed to be a stand up guy, well respected; he did not appear to have lifted a finger to help move things along. Finally, in September, I jumped my chain of command and called Lieutenant Junior Grade Hubbell, our Public Affairs Officer (PAO) directly, to request information about getting my book vetted through the chain of command. I got no response. In fact, I tried from September through the following May to get ahold of LTJG Hubbell, with no success. I left message after message, after message, all to no avail. Then, on June 17, 2011, I received an email from Master Chief Black advising me to send the manuscript to Naval Special Warfare Command (NSWC) PAO again, but cc our legal division, the JAG as well. NSWC and JAG were new points of contact for me, but I'd been trying to reach LTJG Hubbell, our PAO, for a *year* already, and they worked in the same building!

Not wanting to make a stink, I went ahead and sent over my manuscript (again!). This is the email I sent:

Ma'am,

I have spoken to my chain of command but not officially with you. I would like to understand where else I need to go with this process to publish. I have read the guidance email that was sent to me by my MC and have essentially understood that I send it to you and you send it to all the appropriate categories. I need to confirm for my records that you have:

1. received my manuscript.

2. are forwarding it or if you would like me to.

3. what is the time line for this being completed.

If you could get back to me at your earliest convenience I would appreciate it. My SOCS has also been CC'ed on this email for records sake.

V/R

SO1 Carl Higbie

NSW JTAC

DET LC AIR OPS

On June 20th, 2011, she responded, addressing me by my rank, Special Operations Petty Officer 1st Class, or SO1 for short.

SO1,

Your manuscript does not get approved by me, nor do I need to review your manuscript (which I never did receive from you).If you are seeking to publish your book, you will need official DoN review of your manuscript via CHINFO and NAVINFO East.I've attached a guidelines sheet for active duty service members wishing to publish a book.Please ensure you read it and follow the instructions accordingly.

NAVINFO East serves to review book proposals and work directly with CHINFO to determine the amount of support the Navy can offer to the author as well as whether or not approval for support should be granted.For military service members, NAVINFO East should be the Public Affairs Office they contact to begin coordinating review of their material, if it focuses on military and military experience, legal publication.

NAVINFO East, 805 Third Avenue, 9th Floor, New York, NY 10022

R/LTjg Leslie Hubbell

Public Affairs Officer

Naval Special Warfare Center

If you're at all confused by this response, then you're having the appropriate reaction. LTJG Hubbell was the PAO for our Naval Special Warfare Center, the command to which I was attached. In this email, she is explicitly telling me that she is not the one who may say whether or not my manuscript contains classified material or violates OPSEC, but that I must obtain an official Department of the Navy (DoN) review from the UN Navy Chief of Information (CHINFO) headquarters and their regional component, Navy Office of Information East (NAVINFO East). Simple enough, right? Wrong.

Following this email exchange with LTJG Hubbell, I was ordered by Master Chief Dewilde to send my manuscript to all parties listed (CHINFO, NAVINFO East) over unclassified mediums. This struck me as preposterous. Here I was, trying to properly engage with my chain of command to determine whether or not my book contained classified material, and they're telling me to send it through an unclassified channel! This request undermined the entire vetting process, but I did as I was told and mailed a copy of my manuscript to NAVINFO East and to Captain Bill Wilson (who was not listed on the email), Commanding Officer of Naval Special Warfare Command. I was cc'd on an email Captain Wilson wrote to LTJG Hubbell. He addresses her by her first name, Leslie. Superior officers can do that sort of thing.

Leslie,

I would like to have the manuscript sent to PAO and COS WARCOM as a courtesy. WARCOM CDR may be interested in the book as it goes through the vetting process. With the recent publication of books by Greitens and Wasdin, there is interest in any book written by a SEAL.

Thank you,

VR, Bill

CAPT Bill Wilson

CO, Naval Special Warfare Center

So Captain Bill Wilson doesn't really know what's going on either. WARCOM is another command over Naval Special Warfare Command (NSWC). Captain Wilson is saying that he wants the manuscript sent to WARCOM as "a courtesy." He also mentions WARCOM's interest in books written by SEALs, and references Eric Greitens, whose book *The Heart and the Fist: the Education of a Humanitarian, the Making of a SEAL* was published in April 2011, a few months prior to this email. He emailed me personally later on the same day:

> *SO1 Higbie — I have received your book manuscript and will ensure that WARCOM receives it.*
>
> *Thank you.*

So, I've been given assurances by the Commanding Officer of the Naval Special Warfare Center that my manuscript has been received, and will be forwarded onto the next echelon for verification and vetting purposes.

On June 23, I sat through two phone calls with NAV INFO EAST wherein I was told in no uncertain terms that it is not their responsibility to review my book, and that all requests should be routed up my chain of command via the PAO; the same PAO (LTJG Hubbell) who told me that it was not her job to review the book and that I should reach out to NAV INFO EAST! Talk about a *Catch-22*! This is what LT Ferrari at NAV INFO EAST had to say in her follow up email:

> I've attached our DoN Author's memo; we do not review manuscripts here, so please go over the attached with your JAG or ethics counselor.

In the attached author's memo it clearly states that the command JAG and PAO (LTJG Hubbell) are responsible for reviewing the manuscript. If they were attempting to wear me down, it wasn't working.

I was advised, subsequently, to contact Mr. Sean Carney (security manager at NCIS) which I did by phone. He said that the ethics counselor would be in touch with me directly to clear up any misunderstandings. I reported all this to Master Chief Dewilde immediately.

In fact, between June and September I consulted Master Chief Dewilde countless times, and made several attempts to move the process forward, all to no avail. I spoke with Sam Edge, security manager for NSWC Group 2, the body directly underneath WARCOM which oversees the even numbered SEAL Teams. He told me that he did not need to review my book and was unsure as to whether or not that duty fell to the JAG or the PAO or neither, so I got in touch with a family friend who happened to be a federal attorney, as well as an Army Reserve officer. Surely he could help? He wrote the following email on my behalf:

Dear Gentlemen/Madam:

This office represents the interests of PO1 Carlton Higbie in his efforts in a publishing endeavor. I personally have been involved with PO1 Higbie for several years and I am intimately familiar with all of his efforts on our behalf in CONUS and OCONUS.I have been providing him with legal advice regarding all aspects of his career and all aspects of his service abroad, as well as this particular endeavor.

I know that PO1 Higbie has kept his efforts in this publication within the Chain of Command for review, as I have advised him to do. However, at this juncture, in my humble opinion, the Chain of Command has not afforded PO1 Higbie either an adequate or timely response to his request for permission to publish.This has created a scenario whereby he will be both in breach of contract and in default; a situation that I am certain none of us want to occur inasmuch as the negative publicity in that regard may well prove to be embarrassing.

While I am loathe to request that the Chain of Command endeavor to hasten their decision on this effort, I am also loathe to allow the negative impact that a failure to do so will have on PO1 Higbie, his Chain of Command and the Navy.As someone who has spent the majority of his adult life juggling the "Ten Glass Balls of Command" in front line units CONUS and OCONUS, I respect the time and effort needed to "keep those balls in the air" and yet achieve our Admin responsibilities as well.Thus, I ask each of you, on behalf of PO1 Higbie, to redouble your efforts on behalf of PO1 Higbie who needs to live up to the terms of his contract.

I am certain that PO1 Higbie will continue his stellar work within the Team, will lead by example, and continue to trust in his Chain of Command to act on his best interests.Similarly, he has entrusted me to act on his behalf to protect both himself and the Navy from any negative impact that would be attendant with failure to act in a timely manner.The short story is that he has until 30 September 2011 to direct the release of the Publication, which he has entrusted to me and for which I await his release. Thank you for your support.

Very truly yours,

James M. Lenihan, Esq.

Not long after the letter from my pro bono attorney, James Lenihan, was received by Master Chief Dewild, I got an email from the JAG at the Department of the Navy, Head of Security Review with a questionnaire attached:

SO1,

I finished my review of your book.As stated before, I must send my information to WARCOM for an official ethics review. However, prior to sending my review, I need you to complete the enclosed form.Please fill in the sections as completely as possible.Also note that because you reference certain military operations, you need to include an approval letter from DON Security Review Office.In case you are missing that information, I have provided it below.

r/JAG

Mr. David Daley

Head, DON Security Review

CNO(N09N2)/NCIS-24E

Washington Navy Yard, DC

(202) XXX-XXXX"

When I called the number for the DoN Security Review Office, I got a recording informing me that they had relocated to Quantico. There was no forwarding information. And despite Captain Wilson's assurance to me that he had personally delivered my manuscript to WARCOM, they had yet to receive it! Everyone was spinning me round and round in administrative loops, hoping I'd give up and just let it go. In the interest of keeping an unimpeachable record of this whole process, I completed the questionnaire and sent it to Mr. Lenihan. I was subsequently issued a written counseling chit (this is a document the military puts in your record that is typically used for disciplinary purposes) for including a private attorney in the matter and not returning the form to the JAG, Mr. Daley, directly. In the chit it expressly stated that I should not have included an attorney to act on my behalf. This was the command beginning to fear that they were going to be held accountable. For obvious reasons, they didn't want me to have a lawyer.

On September 30, 2011, *Battle on the Home Front* was sent to the printer for final review and production. A few weeks later, on October 10, James Lenihan returned the completed questionnaire to LT Boyd via certified mail. In order to side step any legal snafus, I transferred the rights for my book to an entity, *Ameriman LLC,* which was owned by a family friend. I did this for two reasons: first, I didn't want the Navy to somehow come after the profits of the book, as they perhaps could (and would) if it remained in my name. And secondly, I did it to prove that, for me, it was never about the money.

To cover my ass, I made sure to submit written requests to my chain of command for permission to promote my book through different media outlets. On November 21, I took part in a conference call between Lieutenant Commander Andrew Frontman—OIC of my local command—Master Chief Dewilde, LTJG Hubbel, our command JAG, LT Boyd and a few others who were only marginally involved in the whole process.

I had asked to have my legal counsel present during this call, but was told no. This was obviously a coordinated effort to intimidate and confront me with accusations of treason and bad conduct, sedition, disobeying a direct order, and whatever else they could come up with.

LT Boyd and LTJG Hubbell both denied any wrong doing in their failure to properly vet and route my manuscript up the chain of command, even though the DoN Author's memo LT Ferrari of NAV INFO EAST forwarded me explicitly stated that it was the responsibility of JAG and PAO to do just that. They kept trying to pass the buck to David Daley, the DoN head of security review, whose outgoing message said that his office had moved to Quantico. I couldn't get ahold of him; there was no email address. I didn't even know if he was still employed.

"What am I supposed to do?" I asked them all. "I can't find any information on this guy anywhere."

"We're not here to hold your hand," LCDR Fortman replied smugly. "This is your book, not ours. If you want this project to be completed, you're just going to have to find the information on your own." Then he told me to read *A Message to Garcia* for inspiration, a book first published in 1899 which chronicles the efforts of one man who overcomes great adversity to get a message to another man, Garcia. That was the extent of his "guidance."

I succinctly tried to explain that every single person I had spoken to redirected PAO and me to my command JAG.

"With a all due respect," I said in as respectful a tone as I could muster, "while it is my book, it's *your* approval process that you put in place, and I'm doing everything I can to meet your criteria, but if you don't do your job, that's not my fault and you can't hold me accountable for that."

This was not well received and resulted in another counseling chit for "failing to complete assigned duties." When I asked what those duties were, I was told, "For not completing the review."

With mounting frustration and in the continued interest of completing the review, on November 22, I called NAVINFO East and spoke again with LT (Callie) Ferrari who told me that they (NAVINFO East) in their capacity of security reviewer do not deal with authors directly, and that any pertinent information (including my manuscript) that I might want to share with them should be routed through my command JAG and PAO. This was further confirmation that LTJG Hubbell was dead wrong.

Later that day I received an email from Senior Chief Jones with additional contact information for Mr. Sean L. Carney from NCIS, whom I tried to reach afterwards, but was unable to because Mr. Carney was on leave at the time.

The next day, I spoke directly with Kate Fuster, the head NCIS security review manager (Mr. Carney's superior). I told her about the pushback I was getting from LTJG Hubbell and our JAG, LT Boyd, and she volunteered to play a more active role in things. That afternoon, she wrote me this email:

Mr. Higbie,

Although it is late in the day, I want to ensure there is no confusion over our discussion this afternoon.Contrary to what I have read below, all discussion on this topic will go through me, as I am Mr. Carney's superior and the Branch Head of Security Review for the Navy.I also wouldn't have advised sending the manuscript over unclassified channels if its classification level is in question.If the classification isn't in question, then the manuscript only needs to be reviewed by your Public Affairs Office.Regardless, as I stated to you during our conversation, and because of your active duty status, any such manuscript that contains details of your operational work must be vetted through your command leadership and Public Affairs Office prior to publication.Once again, please direct any questions or correspondence on this matter directly to me when coordinating with my office.

Regards,

Kate Fuster

Branch Head, Security Review

Naval Criminal Investigative Service

There she is lecturing me about sending my manuscript via unclassified channels when it was LCDR Fortmann (and earlier, Master Chief Dewilde) who told me to send it that way! I cc'd most of my chain of command on a subsequent email I wrote to Ms. Fuster and Mr. Carney explaining the precarious position I'd been put in, and included a copy of my manuscript:

Ms. Fuster and Mr. Carney, Despite our conversation today when you (Ms, Fuster) specified that it was not necessary for me personally to send my manuscript to your office, I have been instructed by my chain of command to do so. Attached is the final copy of my manuscript. I have cc'd my entire chain of command who is involved on this email. In addition, when Mr. Carney returns could you pass my contact info to him to sort the rest of this out? Thank you for your time.

Carl Higbie

Master Chief Dewilde was not impressed:

Carl, you need to learn proper ethics with email. You are embarrassing yourself repeatedly. If you would like a sounding board before you transmit to the "World" I would be glad to help you.

Again way too much Command involvement for your private endeavor here. Handle the situation and do what is required. r/W.

So, I wrote back:

Master chief, while I sincerely do appreciate the offer, at this point I am going to elect to have my attorney act and speak on my behalf in the interest of progress.

Carl Higbie

This was tantamount to a nuclear option. I had effectively insulated myself from the legal authority of the military. I was still under contract, and required to obey lawful orders (which I always did, without question, my entire military career). But by invoking my legal rights and involving my attorney in all things *Battle on the Home Front* related, I had made it impossible for them to take legal action without including my legal team in the process. My attorney, Jim Lenihan, was high profile and well respected in the legal field; a much bigger gun than the command JAG, LT Boyd, and they knew it.

At the heart of this whole struggle is the fact that they didn't want my book to be published, but they had no legal recourse to prevent me from getting it out there. So, they did their best to make things difficult or arduous for me, hoping I'd abandon the whole project. But there was no going back. I'd been on two combat deployments, I'd risked my life for my country (and would again, in a heartbeat). I believed that my voice mattered, and I wanted to go on record stating what I think is wrong with the country, and offer suggestions that I thought might get us back on track. It was my right as a citizen to exercise free speech. So long as I didn't attempt to speak for the military or the Special Warfare community in an official capacity, I was well within my rights to speak my mind, or to publish what I wrote.

In the last days of November, I received another counseling chit from LCDR Fortmann for failing to obtain a security review for my manuscript, so I filed an 1150 complaint (one of the few legal recourses an enlisted person has against an officer) against LT Boyd and LTJG Hubbell for their deliberate obfuscation of the review process. Ironically, I then immediately got approval from Commander Freischlag to appear at a Tea Party group rally in Dallas. My request had, at that point, been sitting on his desk for two months.

In December, I was written up two more times for extraneous bullshit. I had, up to this period, never received a single counseling chit in my whole career. I was a decorated SEAL with significant combat experience, and the command was doing all it could to punish me for my decision to publish a book.

On December 3rd, I received the official review of *Battle on the Home Front* from LT Boyd. It was nothing more than a preformatted three-page review with a phrase in one of the boxes that read, "There are potential ethical and UCMJ violations contained in this manuscript." There was no guidance for a path forward. On the advice of my legal counsel I wrote the following email:

> *Gentlemen,*
>
> *Thank you for the review. I do understand the potential for legal action against me, however, I have chosen to continue to publish as is and we have begun the final publication process. Thank you again for your efforts.*

At this point, I'd already directed the final steps of the publication and was going forward, no matter what. This was clearly stated in a letter from my attorney, but still, they didn't get it. By their own rules, I'd given them almost two years to review it and now for the sake of covering their own asses, they submitted a review after the book was being published. I had to put my foot down somewhere. It was now Carl Higbie vs. the US Navy and their infinite resources.

To their credit, on December 7th, I was cc'd on an email from the Security Review Branch Head of NCIS, Kate Fuster to LT Ferrari of NAV INFO East, explaining in detail the protocol for reviewing a book. Finally, after nearly two years of trying to get proper guidance for this process, someone (Kate Fuster) who actually knew what the hell they're talking about laid it out pretty clearly:

> Callie,
>
> Here is the information I promised. 2 of the attachments are information I found personally in my research.The information stated below is taken directly from the SECNAV Manual governing the review process (also attached above).Sorry for the delay, I hope you had a great weekend. Please let me know if you have any questions.
>
> See the information below taken directly from SECNAV M-5510.36 regarding pre-publication. In the event a Manuscript falls under paragraph 2, any/all paragraphs in question must be identified,

so my office can contact the Original Classification Authority (equity owner) to validate the classification of the information in question.

8-8 PREPUBLICATION REVIEW

1. It is DoD policy under reference (r) that a security and policy review shall be performed on all official DoD information intended for public release including information intended for placement on publicly accessible websites or computer servers. Documents proposed for public release shall be first reviewed at the command level as required by reference (s) and may be found suitable for public release without higher-level consideration.

Commanders are authorized to release information to the public that is wholly within the command mission and scope. Each commanding officer is responsible for ensuring that a review of material proposed for public release is completed. This responsibility is normally delegated to the Public Affairs Officer. The security review is part of the overall public release process and is coordinated by the security manager in consultation with command subject matter experts.

2. If public release cannot be authorized within the chain of command, the material must be submitted for further review to the CNO (N09N2) or to the Commandant of the Marine Corps (ARS) (for Marine Corps matters). Exhibit 8B is an excerpt from reference (t) identifying official DoD information prepared by or for DoD personnel and proposed for public release that requires further review by the DoD Office of Security Review (OSR) via the CNO (N09N2). DoD OSR coordinates prepublication review with the cognizant authorities outside the DON and provides the final determination for public release.

EXHIBIT 8B

CATEGORIES OF INFORMATION WHICH REQUIRE REVIEW AND CLEARANCE BY THE DOD

OFFICE OF SECURITY REVIEW PRIOR TO PUBLIC RELEASE

1. Certain categories of information require review and clearance by the DoD Office of Security Review via CNO (N09N2) before public release. They include information which:

a. Originates or is proposed for public release in the Washington, DC area. This requirement applies only to senior level personnel, e.g., flag officers and SES, on a politically or militarily sensitive topic;

b. Is or has the potential to become an item of national or international interest;

c. Affects national security policy or foreign relations;

d. Concerns a subject of potential controversy among the DoD components or with other federal agencies;

e. Is presented by a DoD employee, who by virtue of rank, position, or expertise would be considered an official DoD spokesperson;

f. Contains technical data, including data developed under contract or independently developed and controlled by the International Traffic in Arms Regulation (ITAR), that may be militarily critical and subject to limited distribution, but on which a distribution determination has not been made; or,

g. Bears on any of the following subjects:

(1) New weapons or weapons systems, significant modifications or improvements to existing weapons, weapons systems, equipment, or techniques.

(2) Military operations, significant exercises, and operations security.

(3) National Command Authorities; command, control, communications, computers, and intelligence; information warfare; and computer security.

(4) Military activities or application in space; nuclear weapons, including nuclear weapons effects research; chemical warfare and defensive biological warfare; and arms control treaty implementation.

Kate Fuster

Naval Criminal Investigative Service

Branch Head, Security Review

If that email seems litigious and overbearing to the lay reader, bear with me. I'll make it as painless as possible. Basically, Kate invalidated everything that LTJG Hubbell and LT Boyd said to me over the phone and via email. Both of them insisted that the command PAO and JAG were not required to review a book written by someone under the command. Kate had come to my rescue. She even cited the Secretary of the Navy (SECNAV) manual, chapter and verse. I, of course, knew this all along, but it felt good to be vindicated by someone as well respected and high ranking as Kate Furster.

In January, I was told by Sam Edge, the Naval Special Warfare Group 2 Security Organizer that there was a "potential security issue with a single line on page 102" of *Battle on the Home Front,* and that it should be reviewed by the command JAG (LT Boyd). Nothing ever came of it; I knew better than to disclose security-related information. Nevertheless, I went to Sam's office, where he pulled the line out of the book and said "here," referring to the following sentence:

"Let's take for example, the gate and the outer wall guards on my last deployment to Iraq. At the outer gate there were Marines that were not even allowed to keep their weapons loaded; they maintained what is called 'Condition Three.'"

After I read it aloud, I looked up at Sam and asked, "Yeah...what's the problem?"

"Well, Carl, WARCOM wanted to flag this as it might endanger the troops."

I'm sure you're thinking the same thing I was at the time. Aside from the facts that one; this information was readily available on Google, and two; we had pulled all of our troops out of Iraq by this time, rendering that information completely useless, me saying it wouldn't have endangered the troops nearly as much as *not letting them keep their guns loaded in a combat zone in the first place!*

"Sam, gimme a break. Maybe if they were worried about that, they should have changed the policy. And the last time I checked, we didn't have any troops in Iraq, so what troops are endangered here?" I asked in a snarky tone.

"Look Carl, they just told me to bring this to your attention and let you know that they think this is a security violation, I'm just the messenger here. I see your point but it sounds like you pissed someone off way up the flag pole."

"Okay, thanks. But you do realize that I sent this in two years ago and they could have told me this then, right?" He had no comment.

The command had previously had a problem with my book's subtitle, *A Navy SEAL's Mission to Save the American Dream*, so I had subsequently taken out the "Navy SEAL's" part and replaced it with "Patriot." I realized that it was heavy handed and rhetorical, but that's what I was going for. I wanted it to convey a sense of urgency. At first, I agreed to change it, but in light of the release of the movie, *Act of Valor*, I decided to keep it the way it was. And I informed my chain of command of the decision:

> *Dear Sirs:*
>
> *I have been advised by Counsel that after further and closer review of the ethics and standards that my command has set forward to me, I have decided to revert to the previous subtitle to my book cover*

from "a patriot's mission to save the American dream" to "a Navy SEAL's mission to save the American dream."

My legal team has found no basis for LT Boyd's statement that it was illegal for me to use that subtitle and that after due diligence with respect to the regulations and the codes provided, we are reverting to the previous subtitle.

I have attached the ethics guidance that was provided to me and in addition, the article that supports my decision is as follows:

"F. Misuse of Position Subpart G of the Standards of Conduct prohibits an employee from misusing his official position. Specifically, this subpart prohibits:

• the use of public office for private gain,

• the use of official time, including a subordinate's time, to perform non-official duties,

• the use of Government property for unauthorized purposes, and

• the use of nonpublic information to further a private interest. See 5 C.F.R. §§ 2635.702 - 705. These limitations apply even when an employee may otherwise receive."

"(ii) Appearance of Governmental Sanction/Reference to Official Position. In addition to the prohibitions discussed above, an employee may not use or permit the use of his title or position in a manner suggesting that the Government sanctions or endorses his outside writing."

This information can be found on page 25-26 of the Document attached.

V/R

SO1 Carl Higbie

NSW JTAC

DET LC AIR OPS

I had planned a media tour to coincide with the release of *Battle on the Home Front*, and in the beginning of March 2012, the NSWC command I was attached to made me sign a document stating that "ALL media events likely to garner national attention must be routed through SOCOM [Special Operations Command] PAO."

SOCOM is the command under which all Special Operations, including all the SEAL Teams, Army Special Forces (Green Berets), Marines Special Operations (MARSOC), and Air Force Para Rescue (PJs). Because I had filed an ethics complaint against our command's PAO, I was not to have any interaction with her.

The SOCOM Commander at the time, Admiral William McCraven, who (despite the public's perception, is not well respected inside the SEAL community), reported directly to the president. I'm not sure if this was standard protocol or if they just wanted to add this hurdle because they wanted to make things more difficult, but it added a layer of bureaucracy.

As it turned out, the leave chits that I filed in order to promote my book were all denied by CDR Freischlag who didn't even bother forwarding them up to the SOCOM PAO. So, on March 28th, I filed an article 138 — Complaint of Wrong Against a Commanding Officer. Article 138s are disastrous to the careers of commanding officers, so this one was taken very seriously. On a conference call with my attorney, Mr. Lenihan, LT Boyd offered a quid pro quo: If I withdrew my Article 138, he'd get my leave chits approved. So, I wrote an email accepting the terms of the agreement:

> Respective Sirs, Master Chiefs and chain of Command,
>
> After discussing the conversation between LT Boyd and my attorney James Lenihan and matters regarding the Article 138 I recently submitted with my counsel, I have decided that LT Boyd's statement to approve my media tour pending the withdrawal of my complaint is a fair redress of my grievance.
>
> At this time I, Carlton Higbie, would formally like to withdraw my Article 138 against CDR Freischlag. I want to thank the chain of command for their effort for redress.
>
> V/R
> SO1 Carl Higbie
> NSW JTAC
> DET LC AIR OPS

Only, LT Boyd changed his tune once everything was on paper:

SO1 Higbie,

I was just forwarded the below email by your chain of command. I believe there may be a miscommunication regarding my conversation with your attorney, which I will try to clear here.

I spoke briefly with your attorney on 30 March 2012. I informed Mr. Lenihan that a request for approval for a media tour, which may garner national attention, requires that you the requestor provide the command with specific information. The command needs all the details regarding the event(s) in order to prepare their endorsement. This information is important and necessary because such requests are ultimately forwarded to the Combatant Commander. It is reasonable to inform your CO prior to him endorsing such a high level request.

Based on this, I informed your attorney that if you provided specific information in writing, such as dates, times, locations, topics, media outlet POC's, anticipated topics, etc, that such a request would be endorsed and forwarded to the component commander. For example, prior to your speaking engagement at the Tea Party event, you provided the command specific information. This information allowed the command to properly counsel you on the potential pitfalls of such an event. Such counseling is provided for your benefit to ensure compliance with regulations.

There was no agreement between the command and your attorney. I informed your attorney that if you submitted a complete request, it would be forwarded immediately to WARCOM. That is the only appropriate course of action under the SOCOM PAG. In any event, such an agreement is beyond the control of the command to make. All approval decisions for national media tours must be routed to SOCOM. ATC cannot grant approval, only SOCOM can.

Bottomline, please submit to your chain of command, a complete request for your appearances. Upon receipt, the command will comply with your original request to have those requests forwarded. At this point, the command will consider your article 138 complaint withdrawn.

r/ JAG

LT J. Justin Boyd

SJA, NSWCEN

Because media appearances are often booked with less than twenty-four hours notice, it was impossible to provide them with a detailed list, so I reinstated my complaint:

LT Boyd,

After the last few email exchanges, I would like to confirm the active process of my article 138 complaint against CDR Freischlag submitted 26 March 2012. If there are any issues please let me know. Thank you.

V/R

SO1 Carl Higbie

NSW JTAC

DET LC AIR OPS

Then he wrote back:

> *SO1,*
>
> *Based on your letter which the command received on 9 April 2012, in which you state your desire to submit your letter of 26 March as a complaint pursuant to Article 138, your complaint is being processed pursuant to the rules contained in the JAGMAN.*
>
> *r/ LT Boyd*

It very much became a tit-for-tat type thing, which was not at all how I had ever conducted myself operationally. I always did what I was told, *always.* But when it came to the publication and promotion of this book, the command went out of its way to make things difficult, and I, in kind, began keeping meticulous records, took on outside help from an attorney, and became a tedious, if not recalcitrant man. But, what else could I do? This was the game they wanted to play, so I played along, dug in deep and stood my ground, which, ironically, is what they trained me to do. I finally got a leave chit approved for April 23rd through the 29th. But, on April 19th, it was again revoked, and, frustrated, I sent the following email:

> *Subject: Book: "Battle on the Home Front" and redress of grievances associated*

Respective Command personnel,

In regards to the subject of my recent book and potential punitive action for publishing "Battle On The Home Front":

Sirs, Ma'ams and Chiefs, I have been taught and indoctrinated in a career of honor and commitment. Defending this country against all enemies, foreign and domestic is our battle and I will not quit. I love my Country and the Military and I will exercise my rights endowed by our creator to protect it. I am greatly concerned for the direction of our nation and how our rights and liberties are being revoked in the name of authority. We are all fighting for the same thing: America, Freedom, and the Constitution. I am not asking for your help but rather asking that you observe my constitutional rights and expressed commitment to our nation by ceasing your resistance.

After consulting with Naval and Civilian counsel, I was advised to write this letter in response to my leave being revoked for period 23-29 APR 2012. In a long line of clashes with leadership regarding my book, This is my request for redress regarding my leave request and subsequent denial to promote my book. I am respectfully requesting in writing, the "5 Ws" on this matter. If there is in fact a pending investigation and that is the reason for revoking the chit, my legal team would like to know what exactly are "the potential UCMJ violations" as has been verbally relayed to me, so we can document them and move forward accordingly. I respectfully urge the chain of command to observe their oath to the Constitution, more specifically, the first amendment and the order to it above the UCMJ in the military.

V/R

SO1 Carl Higbie

NSW JTAC

DET LC AIR OPS

"When we assumed the Soldier, we did not lay aside the Citizen."

— *President*

George Washington

THE END

On April 23rd, 2012 (my birthday), *Battle on the Home Front* was released to the public. I had previously obtained an approved leave chit enabling me to be away from the area for a few days. I was planning on heading back to Greenwich and I'd also made arrangements to appear on the news program *Fox and Friends*, but because my leave chit was subsequently revoked, restricting my movement to within a thirty-mile radius outside the base. So I had to improvise.

On April 24th, Fox News was happy to open a local studio to conduct my national broadcast interview at 6:45 AM, before work. One of the first things I said as the interview got underway was that I was appearing as Carl Higbie, the citizen, not Carl Higbie, representative of the Naval Special

Warfare community. I then went on to talk about the things that I believed were causing our nation to crumble from within: entitlements, high taxes, and an aversion to dealing with terrorist threats. The whole thing lasted a couple of minutes, then I was out of there, on my way to work on time and in the uniform of the day.

When I got there, Master Chief Bass laid into me right away.

"What the fuck were you doing on TV? We told you you couldn't leave the area!"

"I didn't leave the area, I followed orders, Master Chief. I went to a local affiliate station."

"You think you're real fucking smart, don't you?"

"I know that none of you want me going public with what I have to say, Master Chief, but I'm within my rights to represent myself as an individual; a citizen. And that's what I did this morning. If you have any further complaints or wish to charge me, please consult my attorney."

He was pissed off and let me know as much, but there was nothing he could do. And though I hated disappointing my superiors, I had to carry this project through to its conclusion. A lot of people at the command started giving me the cold shoulder. Not everyone, of course, but some. In fact, my dilemma caused somewhat of a division in the community. The upper echelon, higher ranked career officers and senior enlisted hated me because I was making politically incorrect statements in public, and making them look bad. But the door-kicking centurions, the backbone of the Teams, almost all sided with me.

The leadership wanted to get rid of me but couldn't, because I was good at my job. A written review of *Battle on the Home Front* authored by Commander Grant S. Staats said as much:

14 May 12

```
From:   CDR Grant S. Staats, USN
To:     Commanding Officer, Naval Special Warfare Center

Subj:   COMMAND INVESTIGATION INTO THE CONTENT OF THE BOOK BATTLE
        ON THE HOME FRONT

Ref:    (a) JAGMAN

Encl:   (1) Appointing Order
        (2) Summary of sworn testimony of SOCM Stephen Bass
        (3) Summary of sworn testimony of LCDR Andrew Fortmann
        (4) Time Line of Events from SO1 Carlton Higbie - Part 1
        (5) Time Line of Events from SO1 Carlton Higbie - Part 2
        (6) Article 138 submittal against CDR Freischlag from SO1
            Carlton Higbie
        (7) Complaint Letter to CAPT Wilson from SO1 Carlton
            Higbie
        (8) Book review by LT John Boyd
        (9) SO1 Higbie Warnings and Rights Form
        (10) Book titled Battle on the Home Front


2.  SO1 Higbie generally does a good job in his role at DLC when
requested to do so.  [encl 2-3]
```

CDR Staats goes on to make a couple of contradictory statements:

```
    b.  Based on the documentation provided by SO1 Higbie, it is
clear that he and his legal team worked to identify the approval
mechanisms necessary to gain endorsement from the Naval Special
Warfare Community and Department of the Navy for his book
release and media appearances.  Mired in bureaucracy, without
requesting official support, and absent approval, the book was
released and at least one national media appearance took place.
```

In this passage, CDR Staats acknowledges that I went to great lengths to do the right thing with respect to the vetting and review process for my book, but the bureaucratic obstacles made it impossible. He even uses the phrase "Mired in bureaucracy." However, elsewhere in the report, he says I "did not follow guidance from my command."

7.   SO1 Higbie did not follow guidance from his Chain Of Command regarding the procedures for the approval to publish his book or take part in media appearances.   [encl 2-6]

This two-faced account underscores the route problem I was facing. On the one hand, my command did not provide me with guidance or support of any kind for the book, the media appearances or anything. But when I took it upon myself to get things done, they accused me of not following directions! It was a classic case of "damned if you do, damned if you don't." I came into the military toward the end of Bush's first term. My tenure extended through his second term, and through the first term of Barack Obama. I believe that the military has been compromised under Obama's leadership, or lack thereof. And what was happening to me with the pushback I got over *Battle on the Home Front*, what Keefe, McCabe, and Gonzales had gone through in Fallujah with that dirtbag, Al-Isawi, were all expressions of that failure of leadership. We were being sacrificed upon the altar of political correctness. Say what you will about George W. Bush, at least he had our backs. No way, no how would any of this garbage have gone down on his watch. But CDR Staats was a career-centric officer, and he had a new ass to kiss, and so he issued the following judgment upon final review of *Battle on the Home Front*:

Recommendations

1. Reassign SO1 Higbie to a role within the NSW claimancy that requires little responsibility and does not require a security clearance.

2. Convene a NEC review board to determine SO1 Higbie's fitness to continue to be a SEAL based on acute SEAL and Navy ethos infractions.

3. Request the assistance of a Staff Judge Advocate to determine whether SO1 Higbie has committed violations of the UCMJ. In any event, I recommend SO1 Higbie be processed for administrative separation to allow a board to determine whether he is fit for continued naval service.

G. S. STAATS

There are a number of things wrong with these recommendations: first off, CDR Staats is recommending that I be reassigned to a new role, one that doesn't require a security clearance. This is a sneaky, underhanded way of saying that I can't be trusted with classified material or information of or relating to national security, which is insane. *Nothing* I disclosed in my book remotely resembled privileged information. To release such intelligence would put my fellow service members at risk. That would be treason, and I would never, on pain of death, even think about doing something like that. If there were classified material or privileged information divulged in *Battle on the Home Front*, I wouldn't be writing this book right now, I'd be in Leavenworth Federal Prison.

Secondly, he's suggesting that a board convene to determine whether or not I deserve to keep my Navy Enlisted Classification (NEC), which is a clever way of saying he thinks I'm unfit to be a SEAL. I'd like to see how his combat record or even peer review holds up next to mine. What Staats fails to mention is that in order to remove a sailor's NEC—according to Navy regulations—the command must demonstrate that said sailor is incompetent at his job, and by CDR Staats' own admission, "SO1 Higbie generally does a good job at his role at DLC [Detachment Little Creek]."

His third finding is patently absurd. He's calling for a JAG to determine whether or not I committed any violations of the Uniform Code of Military Justice (UCMJ), the legal framework which governs the conduct of all military service members. He knows and I know that I didn't violate any UCMJ statutes; this is more smoke. And finally, he recommends that I be "administratively separated" from Naval service, all for exercising my First Amendment rights!

The truth is, I was an exceptional SEAL. At least the people I served with thought so:

I have had the privilege of working with SO1 Carl Higbie during my participation as a student on two separate occasions in courses offered by Naval Special Warfare Advanced Training Command Detachment Little Creek. These courses were Static Line Jumpmaster and HRST/Cast Master. During both courses, SO1 Higbie proved to be a motivated, professional and knowledgeable instructor. Thorough and methodical in his approach to teaching students how to properly and safely conduct high risk evolutions, SO1 Higbie selflessly volunteered his time and was willing to work late to ensure that everyone received the proper level of instruction. An example of this would be during the HRST/Cast Master COI, I was struggling with learning all the required knots and there appropriate implementation. SO1 Higbie, on more than one occasion, stayed late and worked with me on the mockups to ensure that I was familiar with proper rigging procedures and, thus, helping to ensure my success in the course. More importantly, SO1 Higbie's efforts ensured that I was equipped with the necessary skills to take back to my platoon to ensure safe training in over 30 high risk evolutions with foreign partner nations while deployed to EUCOM.

With a driven work ethic and relentless determination, SO1 Higbie dives head first into any situation he is presented with and excels across the board. I am proud to call SO1 Carl Higbie my friend and a fellow Navy SEAL.

I had been around the Teams for over eight years, been on two combat deployments, and countless hours of conditioning. I'd trained guys, I'd been in positions of leadership. I had made and maintained great friendships that people who've never been to combat could never really understand. People trusted me; they trusted me with their lives. They knew I would always be there for them, when push came to shove. And many of them were there for me, too.

To Whom it may concern,

I have known SO1 Carlton Higbie in a personal and professional capacity for seven years, and in that time he has never wavered as someone of the highest moral value and work ethic. I have served in the SEAL teams for ten years, deploying to combat theaters seven consecutive times, the last five of which as a squadron assaulter with █████, and during that time I've had the benefit of working with some of the most talented, dedicated operators in the United States military. Of those operators, Carl stands out as the rare person who steadfastly practices, without exception, what many preach; keep your word no matter the cost, treat everyone with respect until they prove unworthy of it, and go out of your way to help those that are willing to put forth the effort to better themselves.

I first met Carl while supporting a fourth of July fundraiser benefitting the Naval Special Warfare Foundation in his hometown of Greenwich, CT. The fundraiser was held in this locale primarily because of the healthy local support of the military, as well as the overly generous donations that accompany such steadfast appreciation. As such, the SEAL team that is lucky enough to be chosen for that year's demonstration has a lot riding on keeping the image of the consummate professional alive and well. During our brief time in the city of Greenwich, Carl did just that. Arranging events and meetings, smoothly coordinating timelines and ensuring that the demonstration was viewed by as many attendees as possible through exhaustive networking and public relations. Although not the trip leader, and with no stake in our team's reputation, Carl tirelessly went out of his way and assumed responsibility well above his rank to assure that the trip was a success; for the people of Greenwich, my team, and above all the Naval Special Warfare foundation.

SO1 Higbie is a SEAL of incredible work ethic, strong values, and a man who deeply cares for the Naval Special Warfare community and everything it has stood for: Past, present, and future. His contributions to the teams and it's members stand testament to a talented and devoted operator, who has the full respect of his fellow teammates.

Sincerely,

SOC ████████████
████████████████

To whom it may concern:

I am writing to attest to the character of SO1 (S.E.A.L) Carl Higbie. I have known SO1 Higbie for 10 years not only as a superb operator but also as a man of great integrity, extremely dedicated to his family and as a proud American.

SO1 Higbie is a hard charging, take control upstanding citizen who understands the value of a hard day's work. He knows the importance of keeping not only our military running smoothly but also strives to give his input and be a part of a political society that works and I believe our armed forces as well as our day to day way of life continues to benefit greatly from his participation.

I have served in the United States Navy for 17 and half years as a member of the SEAL community, I have completed 13 deployments throughout my career and I feel that I am very capable of recognizing effective leaders and outstanding operators for our armed forces. I can say without a doubt that it would be a devastating blow to our community if SO1 Higbie is not permitted to continue to share his wealth of knowledge and experience as a SEAL operator with his current rank and qualifications.

SO1 Higbie is a natural leader, but more importantly than that, He has been highly trained and deemed worthy by his country in multiple operations abroad to read a situation without prejudice or personal feelings and making the appropriate call which has always brought distinction upon whatever operation or command he has been affiliated with. He recognizes the value of deferring to a superior, and doesn't take a hit to his pride when he is no longer in charge of something.

As we all know an operator needs to posses the ability to both lead and follow, SO1 Higbie has demonstrated those abilities in all aspects of his life on and off the battlefield. I believe strongly in SO1 Higbie's potential for future progressive development of our military, community and overall way of life that we try so hard to protect and covet, so I hope you will accept this statement as a testament to his - HONOR-COMMITEMENT-COURAGE- that I have had the pleasure of witnessing.

Sincerely,

SOC (S.E.A.L) ▮▮▮▮▮▮▮▮▮▮▮

I gathered up these character statements, not only in response to CDR Staats' review of my book and subsequent recommendation for administrative separation, but to deal with an incident that went down just a few weeks before the release of *Battle on the Home Front*. On the morning of March 26th, I left my house early like I did every workday morning. Only this time I was met by a mob of angry protesters who impeded my forward movement. I had to drive very slowly as they casually made way for mine and other passing cars, banging on the hood and trunk and yelling racial slurs at me and the other drivers just trying to get to work.

It turned out that the protest was in support of Trayvon Martin, the unarmed black teenager who was shot and killed by neighborhood watchman, George Zimmerman. These protestors were out for blood, they didn't care whose. I didn't want to make a scene, so I just drove slowly through the crowd as they continued to yell things at me and beat on my car.

When I got to base, I went into the admin office to take care of some paperwork. There was a TV on broadcasting live footage of the Virginia Beach protest I had earlier driven through. An admin gal, or Yeoman First Class (YN1) asked me if I'd seen any protestors on my way to work. Still enraged at the disrespect I'd endured on the drive to work, I said to her, "Yeah, I've seen them, I wish I ran them over!"

Senior Chief Yeoman (YNCS) Young, who was black, misinterpreted my meaning entirely.

"So, you want to kill black people?"

"No, I didn't say that!"

"Those protestors out there are black, you want to run them over?"

"I want to run over anyone who was banging on the hood of my car when I pulled out of my driveway."

"That's not what you said!"

"No, that is *exactly* what I said!"

Things went downhill from there. YNCS Young accused me of being racist and said some nasty things about white people and the Tea Party. Another Yeoman in the admin area, who was also black, took umbrage at what I had said as well. I argued back, it got pretty heated. Eventually, I left. After about ten minutes, I came back into the space and apologized to YNCS Young, who dismissed my attempt to reconcile. The whole thing got blown way out of proportion, as these situations often do in the military, and the command convened an investigation into the incident. From Young's own statement, it's clear that the command was using this incident as a way to punish me for my book.

5. As a Senior Chief Petty Officer with 21 years of distinguished service, Petty Officer Higbie's personal and professional behavior concerns and disturbs me. Based on all the other issues that the command has with P.O. Higbie;

The last clause in that paragraph is very telling. Senior Chief Young says in no uncertain terms that there are "other issues that the command" has with me. Since he was the leading admin counselor, he had been involved the administrative processes regarding my book for the last two years. I wonder what those other issues could be? This incident was a total smoke screen, a ploy to get me to stand before a Trident Review Board of all SEAL Master Chiefs:

<u>Recommendations</u>

1. Issue a Non-Punitive Letter of caution to YNCS ███████ to ensure he understands that he has a responsibility to uphold Equal Opportunity standards, cannot use potentially discriminatory verbiage in any situation, and that he has a responsibility to deescalate these types of situations.

2. SO1 Higbie should be the subject of a Trident Review Board, in order to determine his fitness to continue holding the SO NEC. Additionally, because he is not fit for continued Naval service, SO1 Higbie should be processed for administrative separation.

3. Ensure all members of NSWATC receive training on what CMEO is, what standards of behavior are expected, and what type of behavior will not be tolerated.

LT Christian Foschi, USN

So, for a heated argument with racial overtones, YNCS Young received a "Non-Punitive Letter of caution" and I was made to stand before a board of Master Chief SEALs and explain why I deserved to remain a Special Operator. It was obvious to anyone with eyes that the command was using this incident as a way to discipline me for publishing and promoting my book.

Master Chiefs from all of the Teams—East Coast, West Coast and overseas—were flown in to take part. Initially, I was told I could call as many character witnesses as I wanted, but a few days before the board was to convene they told me I could only bring two, so I had more than seventy-five SEALs of all ranks, including Commanders, write letters of character reference, and asked Gonzales and Krom to appear on my behalf.

We walked into the room and were surrounded on three sides—front, right, and left—by senior enlisted Navy SEALs seated at long tables. The space had more the feel of a tribal council than a courtroom. In the center of the room were three fold-out chairs which were meant for myself and my two character witnesses, Krom and Gonzales. I sat in the middle seat with my brothers-in-arms on either side of me. Gonzales spoke first:

"I've known Carl a long time, he's a great dude. He was Best Man at my wedding, and the definition of a Best Man is someone who would take care of my wife if something bad happened to me. He's one of the best operators I've ever worked with..."

"Alright, that's enough," Master Chief Walters, the guy running the show, interjected.

Gonzales, dejected, sat back down. Krom was next to speak. He stood up and addressed the board in a loud, unfiltered tone.

"I know most of you on this board. I've been down range with most of you, I went to BUD/S with half of you. I've heard you talk about the same things that are in Carl's book. The Teams are falling apart; America's falling apart. At one time or another in your careers, I've heard you all agree with him." He pointed to me, but didn't take his eyes off the Master Chiefs. "You've got these shiny new buildings, and you can't get anyone to stay in, because of this bullshit. This politically correct bullshit."

Krom was referring to the new buildings that had just been put up at Little Creek in the political aspirations of doubling the number of SEALs and to the staggering number of us who had recently gotten out of the service.

"Alright, Krom. That's enough," Master Chief Walters growled. But for Krom, it wasn't enough.

"Why do you think you guys are Master Chiefs and I'm still a 1st Class? It's because I refuse to play the game. I speak my mind, even if what I have to say is unpopular. And it's saved lives. Carl is no different, and you're throwing him under the bus for it. You sit around here and harangue him about the SEAL ethos and this other bullshit that was written by some other ass kissing non-warrior. This is honor, laying down in front of the politically correct train with no regard for his own career just to try and fix the problem. You should be ashamed of yourselves."

"Goddamnit, that's enough!" Master Chief Walters thundered.

After that, I stood to say my piece.

"Master Chief Walters, I've sat around a campfire in Baghdad with you when we talked about the same issues that are in this book, and you agreed with me."

"It's not about that, Carl."

"Then what is this about?"

"You know what this is about."

They briefly addressed the Equal Opportunity complaint that Senior Chief Young had filed against me—ostensibly the impetus for the Trident Review Board in the first place—only marginally and in passing. Mostly, they focused on how I was out of line for publishing a book that contained ideas I believed in.

"You're a good SEAL and a hard dude," Master Chief Hitchcock chimed in. He had been an instructor at BUD/S when I'd gone through more than eight years earlier. After I wore a bathrobe to the store on base one morning, he made me fill a five-gallon bucket with sand using only my mouth. It took five hours to complete, and I never wore a bathrobe on base again. "It's this other shit," he held up a copy of *Battle on the Home Front*, "that we can't allow."

It was obvious that Hitch was not excited about being here and was having a hard time throwing me under the bus.

"It's not about *allowing* it," I protested. "It's my *right!*"

"That's the thinking that got you in front of this board!"

"Respectfully, Master Chief, I'm not sure of the reason for this board, but let's be honest. You tried to Captain's mast me more than ten times, and I requested courts martial every time and you guys backed down, because you had no case. You never had a case. The NEC review board convenes if and only if a sailor is deficient in his rate, and you all know that's not the case with me. I have the right to exercise free speech, I can write whatever I want, it has nothing to do with my job!"

"Shut the fuck up, Carl! You signed those rights away, we all did!"

"Not in a private capacity. If you're going to lecture me about the law, you should at least know what the law *is*. What's in my book are my personal beliefs, as an individual. I made that clear in the waiver."

The opening of *Battle on the Home Front* features a declarative statement that the views contained therein are my own and don't represent Naval Special Warfare or the military in general.

"I don't give a shit about any waiver," Master Chief Hitchcock countered. "You don't speak for us."

"I'm not trying to and I shouldn't have to. You all say the same things behind closed doors."

"Alright, that's enough!" Master Chief Peeler squealed. Around the Teams, he was known colloquially as the "Frog

Killer" for the number of Tridents he'd taken for stupid reasons. "We're going to deliberate. Go wait outside. We'll call you when we've made our decision."

Krom, Gonzales, and I went out into the hall and waited. We didn't say anything. What was there to say? I was fuming mad. I thought about everything I'd worked for; the dangerous situations I'd put myself in for my country. I knew they were going to fuck me over, I just knew it. So I sat, silently. An hour or so later, they called me back in.

I entered the room and stood before the council.

"We're going to recommend they take your bird," Master Chief Walters said, referring to the gold warfare pin—an eagle clutching a pistol and Poseidon's scepter— which signified my identity as a SEAL.

"I figured you would. That decision was made before I even walked out the door this morning," I said without emotion.

After that I became a glorified custodian, shoveling dirt, sweeping the gravel parking lot, just as Gonzales, Keefe, and McCabe had done in Qatar. The command locally suspended my security clearance, because to strip me of it entirely required too much of a procedure, and to do so required an actual review of evidence that I had in fact disclosed classified information. The Trident Review Board sent its recommendation to the Navy Personnel Department (NAVPERS) and a few weeks later, I was called into a video conference with Captain Freischlag, Commanding Officer of the Naval Special Warfare Center in Coronado, our parent command.

Master Chief Bass sat next to me at a desk with an open laptop. On the screen was Captain Freischlag. He didn't look pleased.

"We heard back from Millington," he said triumphantly, referring to the Tennessee city in which NAVPERS is located. "You're out of uniform. Take off your bird."

I knew it was coming, but I couldn't quite mentally prepare myself. This gold-plated device symbolized my entire adult life, everything I had worked for, had *fought* for. I unfastened the bird from my uniform and squeezed so hard, the pins punctured my hand, and I slammed it down on the desk. Blood pooled underneath my hand; I was shaking with anger.

"You should be ashamed of yourself, sir," I said to CDR Freischlag. "Instead of trying to fix the problem, you just want to bury those of us that do."

"Also, you can kiss your Honorable Discharge goodbye," he said smugly.

"There's due process for that."

"Yeah, we'll see about that," he said.

"I look forward to a *fair* trial," I said with a grin.

The call ended and Master Chief Bass closed the laptop and turned to face me.

"You have to choose a rate now, Carl."

"What?"

"You're not a SEAL anymore, you have to pick a different job."

"Yeah, that's not happening."

A shit-eating grin appeared on his face.

"Well, then we'll give you the option of getting out early."

"Where do I sign?"

I only had another four months left on my contract, but I was exhausted from the fight. As a result, I had to pay back $7,000 of my reenlistment bonus, and forfeit over two months of paid vacation days I'd accrued over time. A few days later I headed over to Personnel Service Detachment (PSD) to sign and pick up my DD-214 discharge papers. There wasn't enough space on the form to list all the awards I'd received or military schools I'd attended.

And despite what CDR Freischlag had said, they left my NEC (5326) — Combatant Swimmer (SEAL). I later found out that they never actually pulled my NEC and NAVPERS had no record of any submission to do so, which meant they had done it on the sly. The morons couldn't even get that right.

THIS IS AN IMPORTANT RECORD.
SAFEGUARD IT.

ANY ALTERATIONS IN SHADED AREAS
RENDER FORM VOID

CERTIFICATE OF RELEASE OR DISCHARGE FROM ACTIVE DUTY
This Report Contains Information Subject to the Privacy Act of 1974, As Amended.

1. NAME (Last, First, Middle)	2. DEPARTMENT, COMPONENT AND BRANCH	3. SOCIAL SECURITY NUMBER
HIGBIE, CARLTON MILO IV	NAVY-USN	

4a. GRADE, RATE OR RANK	b. PAY GRADE	5. DATE OF BIRTH (YYYYMMDD)	6. RESERVE OBLIGATION TERMINATION DATE (YYYYMMDD)
SO1	E-6	19830423	N/A

7a. PLACE OF ENTRY INTO ACTIVE DUTY	b. HOME OF RECORD AT TIME OF ENTRY (City and state, or complete address if known)
SPRINGFIELD MEPS CHICOPEE, MA 01022-1519	

8a. LAST DUTY ASSIGNMENT AND MAJOR COMMAND	b. STATION WHERE SEPARATED
NAVSPECWAR ATC DET LITTLE CRK	PERSUPPDET LITTLE CREEK VIRGINIA BEACH, VA

9. COMMAND TO WHICH TRANSFERRED	10. SGLI COVERAGE	NONE
COMMANDER NAVY PERSONNEL COMMAND (PERS-912) MILLINGTON, TN 38055	AMOUNT: $400,000	

11. PRIMARY SPECIALTY (List number, title and years and months in specialty. List additional specialty numbers and titles involving periods of one or more years.)	12. RECORD OF SERVICE	YEAR(S)	MONTH(S)	DAY(S)
5326-COMBATANT SWIMMER (SEAL) (6YRS 7MOS) 9568-JOINT TERMINAL ATTACK CONTROLLER (JTAC) (5YRS 3MOS) 9502-INSTRUCTOR (2YRS 5MOS) X X X X X X X X X X X X X X X X X X X X X X X X X X X X X X X X X X X X X X X	a. DATE ENTERED AD THIS PERIOD	2004	04	05
	b. SEPARATION DATE THIS PERIOD	2012	07	08
	c. NET ACTIVE SERVICE THIS PERIOD	08	03	04
	d. TOTAL PRIOR ACTIVE SERVICE	00	00	00
	e. TOTAL PRIOR INACTIVE SERVICE	00	00	00
	f. FOREIGN SERVICE	00	00	00
	g. SEA SERVICE	00	00	00
	h. INITIAL ENTRY TRAINING	01	06	20
	i. EFFECTIVE DATE OF PAY GRADE	2010	12	16

13. DECORATIONS, MEDALS, BADGES, CITATIONS AND CAMPAIGN RIBBONS AWARDED OR AUTHORIZED (All periods of service)	14. MILITARY EDUCATION (Course title, number of weeks, and month and year completed)
JOINT SERVICE COMMENDATION MEDAL W/COMBAT V; NAVY/MARINE CORPS ACHIEVEMENT MEDAL; COMBAT ACTION RIBBON; NAVY GOOD CONDUCT MEDAL(2); NATIONAL DEFENSE SERVICE MEDAL; IRAQ CAMPAIGN MEDAL 01MAR09-15NOV10; GLOBAL WAR ON TERRORISM EXPEDITIONARY MEDAL NOV05; (CONT BLK 18)	RECRUIT TRAINING 8WKS JUN04; STOREKEEPER CLASS A 9WKS AUG04; BASIC UNDERWATER DEMOLITION/SEAL (BUD/S) INDOCTRINATION 5WKS OCT04; BASIC UNDERWATER DEMOLITION/SEAL 15WKS APR05; SQIP, AIRBORNE 3WKS MAY05; SEAL BASIC COLD WEATHER MARITIME 3WKS OCT05; (CONT BLK 18)

		YES	NO
15a. COMMISSIONED THROUGH SERVICE ACADEMY			x
b. COMMISSIONED THROUGH ROTC SCHOLARSHIP (10 USC Sec. 2107b)			x
c. ENLISTED UNDER LOAN REPAYMENT PROGRAM (10 USC Chap. 109) (If yes, years of commitment:	)		x

16. DAYS ACCRUED LEAVE PAID	17. MEMBER WAS PROVIDED COMPLETE DENTAL EXAMINATION AND ALL APPROPRIATE DENTAL SERVICES AND TREATMENT WITHIN 90 DAYS PRIOR TO SEPARATION	YES	NO
60.0			x

18. REMARKS
SER: 42575-12-2294-EMT "SUBJECT TO ACTIVE DUTY RECALL/ANNUAL SCREENING" (BLK 13 CONT) GLOBAL WAR ON TERRORISM SERVICE MEDAL; NAVY SEA SERVICE DEPLOYMENT RIBBON. (BLK 14 CONT) DIVING EQUIPMENT MAINTENANCE AND REPAIR 2WKS DEC05; NSO PARA RIGGING 4WKS MAR06; SEAL ADVANCED CLOSE QUARTERS DEFENSE 1WK APR06; NAVAL SPECIAL WARFARE (NSW) COMMUNICATIONS 6WKS DEC06; NPC FREE FALL 4WKS MAR09; STATIC LINE JUMPMASTER 3WKS NOV09; (CONT DD-214C)

The information contained here in is subject to computer matching within the Department of Defense or with any other affected Federal or non-Federal agency for verification purposes and to determine eligibility for, and/or continued compliance with, the requirements of a Federal benefit program.

19a. MAILING ADDRESS AFTER SEPARATION (Include ZIP Code)	b. NEAREST RELATIVE (Name and address - include Zip Code)

20. MEMBER REQUESTS COPY 6 BE SENT TO (Specify state/locality)	CT	OFFICE OF VETERANS AFFAIRS	x YES	NO
a. MEMBER REQUESTS COPY 3 BE SENT TO THE CENTRAL OFFICE OF THE DEPARTMENT OF VETERANS AFFAIRS (WASHINGTON, DC)			x YES	NO

21a. MEMBER SIGNATURE	b. DATE (YYYYMMDD)	22a. OFFICIAL AUTHORIZED TO SIGN (Typed name, grade, title, signature)	b. DATE (YYYYMMDD)
	20120708	P.C. BRANCH, GS-7, SEPSUP BY DIROIC	20120708

SPECIAL ADDITIONAL INFORMATION (For use by authorized agencies only)	
23. TYPE OF SEPARATION DISCHARGED	24. CHARACTER OF SERVICE (Include upgrades) HONORABLE

25. SEPARATION AUTHORITY	26. SEPARATION CODE	27. REENTRY CODE
MILPERSMAN 1910-102	KCC	RE-3M

28. NARRATIVE REASON FOR SEPARATION
REDUCTION IN FORCE

29. DATES OF TIME LOST DURING THIS PERIOD (YYYYMMDD)	30. MEMBER REQUESTS COPY 4 (initials) CM H
TL: NONE	

CERTIFIED TRUE COPY CM H

DD FORM 214, AUG 2009   PREVIOUS EDITION IS OBSOLETE.   **MEMBER - 4**   Adobe Designer 8.0

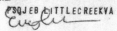

PSQJ EB LITTLE CREEK VA

To my relief, block 24 read "HONORABLE," for the character of discharge. So much for my CO's promise. In the military, there are only two ways to reduce someone's discharge legally if they've been in longer than six years: an administrative separation board (ADSEP) or a court martial. Both of these would have required the command to produce evidence against me to a neutral panel of my peers. They knew that this would be a waste of time, so they dropped it.

And then it was over. I was done. I was able to spend some quality time with my wife, who was now pregnant with my daughter, and try to grow my tree service business. It felt strange not to be connected to Naval Special Warfare; to drive past the base and not be going into work. It wasn't just a job. It was so much more. And had I kept a lid on things, I'd probably still be in. But it's not in me to remain silent, and I care so much about this country that I had to write and publish *Battle on the Home Front*, which sold thousands of copies, and continues to sell, even though it cost me my career. But there's more to life than military service. I had a family, a kid on the way, a prosperous business to run, and a host of great Veterans' benefits for which my Honorable Discharge made me eligible. In a way, I was relieved it was all over. In August, I appeared on Fox News again to promote my book and discuss issues that I felt were negatively impacting the country. Then, a few days later, I got this in the mail:

August 28, 2012

Mr. Higbie,

Enclosed is a DD-215 that was processed at the request of your command. The request is enclosed for your reference.

Please use the DD-215 in conjunction to your DD-214.

Should you have any questions regarding this action, please contact your command directly.

Respectfully,

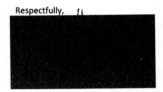

What the fuck is this all about? I wondered. I was already out, I *had* a DD-214 that I signed *myself* at PSD some six weeks earlier. A DD-215, I later learned, is a correction to a DD-214, meaning this new discharge order that I'd received in the mail was somehow different from the one I'd left the service with. The next page of the letter made it glaringly clear what exactly was different about this one:

DEPARTMENT OF THE NAVY
COMMANDING OFFICER
NAVAL SPECIAL WARFARE ADVANCED TRAINING COMMAND
1 HOOPER BLVD
IMPERIAL BEACH, CALIFORNIA 91932-1050

1900
N00
26 Jul 12

From: Commanding Officer, Naval Special Warfare Advanced
      Training Command
To: Officer in Charge, Personnel Support Detachment,
      Little Creek, VA

Subj: DD214 ERROR ICO SO1 CARLTON M. HIGBIE, USN, XXX-XX-████

Ref: (a) My ltr 1910 00 of 2 Jul 12
      (b) COMNAVPERSCOM MILLINGTON TN 081200Z Jun 12

1. Due to failure to comply with reference (a) and guidance
given by reference (b) request DD215 be issued to correct errors
made to subject named member's DD214.

2. Change Blocks 24 and 27 to reflect General and RE-4
respectively.

3. Although Service Member was separated via Reduction in
Force, he received an adverse separation evaluation not
recommending retention due to violations of NAVPERS 1070/13 and
removal of SEAL NEC (5326) due to loss of confidence from the
Commanding Officer.

4. Please direct any questions regarding this matter to my
Administrative Officer ENS ████████████████████████.

W. F. DENTON

Captain Denton, who was CDR Freischlag's superior after I'd left the military, had signed this order to retroactively change the characterization of my discharge from "Honorable" to "General," and strip me of my SEAL (NEC) 5326.

They can't do this! I seethed. *Can they?* I didn't fully understand the content of the letter when I first laid eyes on it, but I knew who would: Guy, the JAG lawyer who'd written the forward to the book and represented Gonzales at that joke of a courts martial in Baghdad. I called him immediately.

"Guy, they took away my Honorable Discharge! They gave me a new DD-214! Can they do that?!"

"Whoa, chill out, Carl! Read me what the letter says."

I read the letter to him, verbatim.

"What the fuck? They can't do that," he said.

"Are you sure?"

"Yes, I'm sure. That violation of NAVPERS 1070/13 is just a regular Page 13, you know, administrative remarks. It's not grounds to change the characterization of your discharge."

"Really?"

"Yeah, and besides, you're already out. You have a copy of the DD-214 you signed when you checked out of the command, right?"

"Yes, it's in the house."

"They can't issue you a new DD-214 when you've already been discharged, it's illegal. They would have to recall you to Active Duty, courts martial you, then issue you a new discharge. They're trying to fuck with you, Carl. You must have really pissed them off with that book. Let me make some calls and figure this out, dude."

"I didn't do anything I wasn't supposed to."

"I know you didn't. We'll get this sorted out."

"Thanks, Guy."

"Dude, you were a SEAL. They can't just take away your Honorable Discharge because you said some things they didn't agree with."

"That's what I've been saying all along."

In the meantime, I was under the assumption that I was unable to use my GI Bill to go back to school, while guys who'd done four months in the Air Force, were never in combat, never even deployed, got full use of their Veterans' education benefits.

It took almost two years, but eventually we unanimously won our appeal. Guy called me from his Pittsburgh office one afternoon and read this letter out loud over the phone:

DEPARTMENT OF THE NAVY
SECRETARY OF THE NAVY COUNCIL OF REVIEW BOARDS
720 KENNON ST SE RM 309 (NDRB)
WASHINGTON NYD DC 20374-5023

FOR OFFICIAL USE ONLY – PRIVACY SENSITIVE
Any misuse or unauthorized disclosure may result in both civil and criminal penalties.

March 28, 2014
ND13-01560/NGA

CARL M HIGBIE IV

███████████████

NOTICE OF DECISION THAT DISCHARGE CHARACTERIZATION CHANGED

The review authority has given consideration to all relevant issues raised and evidence presented and has carefully examined all available official records in connection with your application for discharge review.

The final decision is that the discharge be changed to Honorable.

Enclosure (1) is a copy of the Record of Review of Discharge. This document has been made a part of the official service personnel record.

By copy of this notice and the Record of Review of Discharge, the service personnel manager is requested to issue new discharge documents to reflect the final decision in this case. **Any correspondence regarding these documents should be addressed to Commander, Navy Personnel Command, Department of the Navy** ████████████████████████████████
Please allow at least eight weeks before contacting that office.

J. D. Reeser
J. D. REESER
President, Naval Discharge Review Board

I had stood my ground, refusing to give in. I'd done exactly what I was trained to do: never quit. And with Guy's help we beat the system.

We had beaten the U.S. Navy, the DOD and most of all, the career-centric men that tried to strip me of what I cherished most; honor.

Rarely ever in the history of the Naval Discharge Review Board had the arbiters voted unanimously to restore the characterization of a discharge to "Honorable." The victory is bittersweet. I miss the Teams. Still, sometimes when I close my eyes at night, I can remember sitting in a helicopter, feet dangling out the door. The rumbling sound of the blades as we cut our way back from a gunfight after kicking ass all night is never far from my thoughts. I remember staring down at the tattered American flag patch on my shoulder and thinking, "Freedom isn't free."

I miss being a SEAL. I miss watching guys go from raw warriors to disciplined operators. I miss jumping out of airplanes, and I miss going on night ops and killing bad guys. I miss it all, but if I had it to do over again, I wouldn't have done anything differently. I said what I had to say, because it had to be said. We reinforced a new understanding of the First Amendment for all military service members, became an integral part of how the JAG corps defines service members' first amendment rights, sold thousands of books and ignited a base of support greater than I ever could have imagined. I am humbled, having given speeches on the Washington Monument—overlooking the US Capitol building—in front of thousands. I've made hundreds of media appearances, all to help fuel the fire and energize people to fight for what they believe in and for America. It has been my honor. I love my country more than anything, even more than being a SEAL, and it was all worth it. And I owe it all to the freedoms that we are granted as Americans. So here's to you, to all the men and women who have put foot to ass when your country has called. Let this be a lesson to those that wish to undo or stand idly by and let others undo what has made America great. Better patriots than me will always stand in front of those who seek to destroy what America stands for.

Thank you.

ABOUT THE AUTHORS

Carl Higbie was a Special Operator with SEAL Team Ten, Echo Platoon. He deployed twice in support of Operation Iraqi Freedom. Carl published his first memoir, *Battle on the Homefront* shortly after his second deployment. He is a regular contributor on Fox News. Carl ran for Connecticut's 4th Congressional District in 2014. He resides in Greenwich, CT.

Brandon Caro was a Navy corpsman (combat medic) who deployed to Afghanistan in support of Operation Enduring Freedom in 2006-2007. His first novel, *Old Silk Road*, was published by Post Hill Press. His work has been featured in *The New York Times*, *The Daily Beast*, *WhiteHot Magazine*, and others. He resides in Austin, TX.